ENDORSEMENTS

"This book has great meaning and insight for me as I continue on in my healing after the loss of both my parents. Cheryl has eloquently related the process we go through whenever we experience the loss of a loved one or a loved pet.

"From the first page to the last, this remarkable book captures for the reader the full range of emotions that accompany the loss. In a deeply moving way, Cheryl moves from the pain that the knowledge of impending death brings, through the wrenching experience of losing a loved one and on the path forward from grieving into healing and wholeness.

"*For the Love of Princess* reveals a profound relationship of love, a speaking and listening in truth, the strength and openness and trust, and incredible loyalty and devotion. This is truly a book of love in all its glory, mystery, pain and transformation."

Karen Gipner,
Medford, Oregon

"A powerful, moving love story in lessons of the heart...to the quiet realization that the ultimate test of love is in letting go when the time has come."

Roxanne Hersman,
Seattle, Washington

"I have found this book to be not only helpful in coping with the loss of a pet, but the most beautiful eulogy to a friend that I've ever read. Being an animal health technician for the last ten years, I deal with clients experiencing pet loss almost every week. It's never easy to say goodbye, but I feel Cheryl has captured a very sincere and real feeling that we all seem to share for our pets, but are not often able to put into words.

"Cheryl has dealt with some very real and tough questions in going completely through the loss. I feel anyone with a pet will be able to relate to this book and grow a little more because of it. Thank you, Cheryl, for sharing Princess with us. Her memory lives on with us, too!"

Judy Tate
Animal Health Technician
Portland, Oregon

"This book has something important to say that goes beyond the loss of a loved pet. It speaks to us of loss and suffering without platitudes, empty moralizing or quick answers. Cheryl combines extensive practical experience, psychological insight and deep faith in our ability to move beyond suffering into healing.

"Having lost a canine companion myself, and experiencing all the pain and grief that followed, I could easily relate to and identify with the sensitivity and emotion in every page."

Evalyn Reich,
Aloha, Oregon

"A most beautiful love story! If you've ever loved and lost, you'll be able to relate to this book and find understanding in your grief."

Cecile Hammill,
Clinic Manager
Medford, Oregon

"At last! A book to help us through the devastating pain of separation from our pets that have become a part of the family. You'll refer to it again and again as you experience the loss of loved ones...both human and animal. A wonderful guide for the way to emotional healing.

Delores Kern,
Portland, Oregon

"Realizing that a need exists, Cheryl Kilbourn has written an excellent portrayal of the nature and outcome of grieving. It is written for anyone who has lost a meaningful pet through death and strives to understand that loss.

"I have been there and Cheryl's account of life, death and bereavement are factual. I laughed, I cried and I learned.

Lorraine Alicata
Veterinarian Support Staff Person and Pet Lover
Portland, Oregon

FOR THE LOVE OF PRINCESS

Surviving the Loss of Your Pet

By Cheryl A. Matschek

Princess Publishing, Portland, Oregon

Published by:
Princess Publishing
P. O. Box 25406 • Portland, Oregon 97298• U.S.A.

Selections from Isaiah 43 are taken from The New American Bible, copyright 1970 by the Confraternity of Christian Doctrine, Washington, D.C. Used with permission.

First Printing 1987
Second Printing 1998

Library of Congress Cataloging-in-Publication Data
Kilbourn-Matschek, Cheryl A., 1947 -
    For the Love of Princess.

    1. Pet owners - Psychology.   2. Dog owners -
Psychology.   3. Pets - Death - Psychological aspects.
4. Bereavement - Psychological aspects.   5. Dogs -
Washington (State) - Seattle - Biography.   6. German
shepherd dogs.   7. Kilbourn, Cheryl A., 1947-
II. Title.
SF411.47.K55   1987   155.9'37   87-3109
ISBN 0-943367-07-7 (pbk.)

IN MEMORIUM

On April 17, 1986, Princess passed from this life to be united with the truly beloved. Her death brought much pain, but with the pain has come transformation.

This book is dedicated to Princess...to the memory of life shared with my special companion.

iii

To see in one life such wonder, such anticipation, such incredible awareness has been an extraordinary example for me about what it means to be fully alive. Living with Princess was to live continually in the spirit of inspiration and today, as she dances without restriction, her transformation offers me new inspiration.

The intensity of our relationship, all the moments shared, the remarkable ability we had to communicate and her memory gives my life new meaning with each new sunrise...then and now.

Princess has touched me deeply. I have found that love truly is stronger than death. She gave me much in life and she continues to give me much in death. Our love continues and her song goes on. And I will do the singing.

Thank you, Princess, for loving me through the laughter and the tears...for sharing some of the most beautiful, joyful and painful years of my life...and for being patient enough to help me to work through it all to learn the meaning of love and the essence of living. Without you life would not have been what it was, or be what it is today. Thank you.

TABLE OF CONTENTS

PREFACE

Dear Friend,

While support is normally extended to those who are grieving over the loss of a human family member or friend, all too often that same support is not given to the grieving pet owner after the loss of their pet. And yet it is so greatly needed.

Until now, unless a person was supported by another family member or friend who understood and appreciated the loss, or by a veterinarian who offered a gentle ear, there was little support available. Although support groups are beginning to form in many communities around the country to help answer this need, there has been little written to help the pet owner through the grieving process. And now, at last, this book has been written to help those individuals who must face the death of their loved pet.

Just six months before going through the loss with Cheryl, I experienced the euthanasia of my canine companion, Amos. I, too, felt that same need for support. Although the piercing pain has eased, I still miss Amos. I often think of him and ask him how he is and let him know that he is still a part of my life. That will always be. As I read this book many memories were relived...the happy and sad, the beautiful and painful, but all of them special.

I had the pleasure of caring for Cheryl and Princess during the last four years of Princess' life and I witnessed the deep bond of love and affection they shared. I saw Cheryl laugh, and I saw her cry...and I was there at the end when Princess and Cheryl shared their good byes for the last time.

It is never easy to say good bye when the time has come, especially when it means saying good bye to a beloved companion who has become so much a part of your life, indeed a family member. Euthanasia is a difficult decision to make, yet there comes a time when prolonging the decision causes only more pain for both the pet owner and the pet. Cheryl openly shares the process she went through in making the decision and in being there when Princess was euthanized...a most painful, yet beautiful, peaceful experience.

In this book Cheryl has captured the joy and the pain, the happiness and the sadness of her loving relationship with Princess. She shares this freely with you, the reader, with the hope of helping you through the pain that you will inevitably experience as you face the difficult decision and say your last good byes and the grieving process that follows.

If you have ever shared the special companionship of a loved pet, I'm sure you will find reading this to be most beneficial. And, if you've lost your love and haven't fully healed, this may be the next step toward healing. I hope that it is.

David A. Barno, DVM

David A. Barno, D.V.M.
Rock Creek Veterinary Hospital
Aloha, Oregon

INTRODUCTION

It is difficult to put into words a relationship that developed over nine years and one month. Years of loving, sharing and bonding...beautiful years that time can never erase; feelings that run deeply into the core of my being. Princess was more than a special dog; she was my child, my best friend. She was always there, always loving and accepting, freely and unconditionally. And now she's gone from this life, and how do I cope? How do I adjust? Those were the questions I painfully asked myself as I began my journey into recovery and healing from her loss. Years of togetherness, sharing some of the most difficult and some of the best years of my life, was replaced with an emptiness that I thought would have no end.

Writing this wasn't easy and there have been thousands of teardrops poured over my drafts. Tears of pain, tears of love. But I've persisted for three reasons. First, for Princess...as a tribute to her, my gentle, loving companion who taught me so much about life and living. Second, for me, because I needed to do this for myself. It has actually been part of my healing process and has helped me gain some closure. But perhaps most of all for you...for those who will someday have to face a similar experience of letting your beloved pet "go home"; for those who have already experienced such a loss, but have been unable to move through the healing process completely. And for others who have never shared the love of a pet, but want to understand more deeply their friends who have.

For all those who love as I have loved, for all those who have developed that special bond with their pet, I share my experience openly with the hope that it will bring you the peace, joy and hope that I have found, and a lasting memory of a shared love that will never die.

Cheryl

PART I

THE JOURNEY HOME

Many children grow up with a dog, cat or some other pet and I was no different. We had a family dog, Tweedy; my brother had a chipmunk, Dale; and I had my very own golden mantle squirrel, Chippy. Recalling those childhood years brings back many special memories of my family and our pets, but as much as I loved our animals, it was different then. We all shared in the companionship and we shared in the responsibilities of caring for them. It wasn't, however, until I was grown, moved from Medford, Oregon, to Seattle, five hundred miles away from my family and had my very own pet and all the responsibilities, that I understood the incredible companionship and love that can be developed with a pet.

She was my buddy, my best friend. I loved her, and she loved me and we communicated more like two people than a person and a dog. We were like a tree and its roots, one a part of the other. When I looked at her, I saw a part of me; when I looked at myself, I saw a part of her. During our years together we had grown inseparable; we had joined souls. I treated her more like a human than a dog and she responded accordingly. We talked to each other and discussed everything from business plans to vacation schedules, from what to fix for dinner to how to solve a problem. Our conversations revolved around life and love and the meaning of it all. She taught me what it really means to be alive, to love fully. She became such a part of me that I couldn't imagine ever living without her. Then one day, nine years and one month after she became "family" and stole my heart, she was gone.

What follows is my story, but it is more than a story. It is about companionship and bonding, about loving and letting go, about life and death and eternity. It is a tribute to the love we shared...the love between a woman and her canine companion. This is how it all began.

Friday, March 18, 1977. Just five days before, I had arrived home from work at the same time burglars were making their escape from the sliding glass door in my dining room. The police had returned for a somewhat unusual follow-up visit two days after the burglary incident to speak with me about security. They suggested that I consider some kind of protection and talked about the value of a burglar alarm system or possibly a dog. Today I would follow their advice. I was going to get some protection and it wouldn't be an alarm system. I was going to get me a puppy, and my mind was racing with enthusiastic anticipation.

Karen, a close friend of mine, came to visit from Southern Oregon, and I had taken the day off from work so we could accomplish our mission. Another friend and business associate, Paul, was going to chauffeur us to the kennels. He had convinced me that a German Shepherd was what I needed, so off to the purebred German Shepherd kennels we went.

I remember feeling like a little kid at Christmas, with excitement mounting as we headed for the kennels. Entering the long driveway into the kennel area, I could hardly believe my eyes. Looking back, it seemed there were hundreds of German Shepherds covering acres of land. I had never seen so many dogs all in one place. How would I ever be able to choose just one?

Ann, the kennel owner, took me to the mother and father of the newest litter to meet them before introducing me to their seven-week-old puppies. After making their acquaintance, we walked toward the puppies' kennel where I was about to make a decision and enter into the ranks of motherhood. I can still see it just as vividly today, ten years later. There she was...my Princess. *My Princess*...and I knew it. As I knelt down to get closer to the little bundle of fur, I knew this was the puppy that would soon be making her home with me. Dancing excitedly, putting her paws through the chain link fence that separated us, and squeezing out all the other puppies was the little girl who would become my constant companion and my very best friend. Eyes glistening, tail wagging faster than the speed of light, yelping as if to say, *"Choose me, Mom, I'm yours,"* was all I needed to make my decision. At that moment, I became a mother.

As I held her in one arm, awkwardly writing out the check with my free hand, Ann versed me in the basics. I was so excited and preoccupied with the little bundle in my arms that I'm not sure I heard much of what she said. Fully understanding my lack of attention to her comments, Ann invited me to call if I had any questions or problems. I do, however, remember one thing she said. "She has just eaten (cottage cheese and hard boiled eggs, I was soon to find out), and the excitement may be a little much for her right now." I think that was meant as a warning.

Paul, Karen, Princess and I piled into the car to begin our journey home. Karen and I decided to sit close together and lay Princess across each of our laps so we could both hold her. Karen, trying to anticipate any possible problems, said, "I'll take her head, you take her tail end." (She thought it would be safer.) I'll never forget that moment, and neither will she. A few miles down the road, Princess' excitement turned into one of those unforeseen events as she threw up all over Karen's white slacks and onto the upholstery of Paul's car. As Paul pulled into the nearest service station so we could clean up the mess, Karen sat there bewildered and Princess continued wagging her tail as if nothing had happened. The rest of the trip was uneventful except for the roaring laughter as we recalled Ann's words of warning and Karen's attempt at getting at the safe end. Our next stop...home.

As we began making Princess' place in our home, I realized that I had forgotten to buy a clock. After all, I had always heard that the ticking of a clock would quiet a new puppy. So, a clock for Princess it was, and off to the store we went, leaving Princess in the garage while we were gone. We returned with clock in hand, along with some toys, a dog dish and a few unessential extras that I couldn't pass up for my little girl.

Back home that night, we spent hours playing and talking, telling Princess all about her adoption and that she was home to stay. And naturally as any proud parent would do, I began taking pictures for her own private photo album. Pictures taken of Princess and her first night at home are so special to me today. They now serve as a memory of those first hours together, and the great anticipation and expectations of the wonderful life that was to be shared in the years ahead. Our life together was just beginning.

MUTUAL AGREEMENT

Princess and I had reached an understanding. She stayed in the garage during the day while I worked and spent the rest of the time in the house with me when I was home. At least I thought we had an understanding, until...

Well, suffice it to say she didn't like the garage and she was trying her best to let me know how much she disapproved of the arrangement. One evening I arrived home to find my childhood doll and cradle (which had been neatly packed in a box and stored in the garage) opened rather untidily and strewn all over the garage. Arms out of sockets, hair torn off, the remains of my doll were scattered about the garage floor like confetti. And I was angry. That was the first time I questioned whether or not that cute little bundle was a wise decision...to make her a part of my life, that is. Nevertheless, this too shall pass, and it did. All it took was a wag of her tail, a gaze of those big brown eyes, her chin resting beside me on the couch as I sat looking at her...and I melted. "Yes, Princess, I love you. I don't like what you did, but I love you anyway." Just like talking to a child!

I had a strange feeling that if I let her stay in the house during the day it would be safer, but I wasn't ready to trust my gut feelings. She never chewed on anything in the house...not furniture, clothes, stuffed animals, nothing. Sometimes I wondered if she wasn't really a human rather than a dog. She had such a good temperament and never did anything destructive like I had heard puppies sometimes do.

Actually, I finally gave in. I thought she would enjoy being in the house during the day, and after all she was to guard the house, wasn't she? So we gave it a try and from the very first day she was remarkable. No messes, no chewing; she was a perfect lady. So ended her days in the garage. Now Princess would meet me at the door wagging her tail as soon as I entered the house each night. What excitement! So happy to see me, she alternately jumped up on me to say hello and wagged herself into circles. What a pleasure. Coming home was fun now and I wasn't lonely anymore. The once empty house was always filled with life and my very best friend.

PERSONALITY PLUS

Unlike human babies who don't seem to have much personality for the first few weeks of their life, my child seemed to be born with her personality fully developed. Charm, coyness, spunk, strong will...but always loving, very loving. She needed attention, she wanted attention and she knew how to get it.

Princess was so frisky and had an unlimited source of energy. Some days when I was extremely busy she was so playful and persistent for my attention that I would become aggravated and feel guilty about it later. These were the times I looked forward to the end of the puppy stage when she would quiet down, but I was often reminded by friends that children grow up all too quickly and the childhood years would soon be held in memory only. Instinctively I knew this was true, and I rapidly came to fully appreciate her puppyness, even when her energy exceeded mine. Actually, she maintained that puppy attitude and behavior in many ways up to the last days. In fact many people, including her veterinarian, thought she still looked and acted like a two or three-year-old when she was eight.

Like most children, Princess delighted in showing off and she loved to be the center of attention. On numerous occasions she would put on her own private show for anyone in viewing range. She was the producer, director and the show itself. Trying to put into words her antics is virtually impossible, but she captured the attention of all present and elicited laughter from her audience. Regardless of the conversation we "adults" might be having, she determined when the show was to begin and she began without any introduction. As if to say, "Thank you, I appreciate your applause and attention," her finale consisted of casually making the rounds of everyone present to receive their pat of affection and approval then finding a spot close by to listen to the rest of the conversation. She loved to be with people and insisted upon it, almost as though she was afraid of missing out on something important.

I had always been told that animals can sense people who fear or don't like them, and that the animal would avoid or back away from them. Not Princess. If we had a visitor over to our home who was afraid of large dogs, she always made her way to them first. Princess knew no stranger and wanted everyone as her friend.

One December after Princess and I had moved to Portland, Mom and Dad were coming to visit for a couple days so Mom could attend a business meeting in town. I had decorated the house for Christmas and since the only fireplace we had was a free-standing fireplace with no mantle, our stockings were hung on the wall. I decided to put Princess' small toys in her Christmas stocking while she was outside playing and couldn't see me. I don't know how she figured out they were already in the stocking, but by the time Mom and Dad arrived and Princess came inside, she headed straight for the wall. What followed was perhaps the most unforgettable theatrical presentation of all.

It began with Princess quietly laying on the floor directly under the stocking, gazing uninterruptedly at her find. A few minutes later she was sitting, neck stretched out as far as it could stretch upward. Calling Princess to break her attention and get her away from the stocking elicited absolutely no response. If she heard us, we didn't have a clue. She wasn't for a moment going to break her surveillance. As we began laughing and our laughter grew louder and louder, Princess jumped up and rested her paws on the wall, eyes darting between us and the stocking, back and forth, back and forth. She had one thing on her mind. Toys. Right now, not December 25. As we continued laughing, she exhibited what seemed to be utter frustration at our inappropriate behavior and began letting us know with her whining and yelping. She meant business and she wasn't planning to wait until Christmas to achieve her objective. To put it mildly, Princess carried on for several minutes as we watched on in amazement at her persistence. Finally, for her peace of mind and our peace and quiet, she got what she wanted and Christmas began a few weeks early.

Unquestionably, Princess did have a personality. In fact, she had enough for herself and all the other German Shepherds where she came from. Day by day something new was added making our life together quite an adventure with hardly a dull moment. Since she loved to have her pictures taken, we spent numerous hours pushing the camera button and saying, "Smile, Princess, say 'cheese.'" I thought it was only proud grandparents that bought rolls and rolls of film to capture the years of growing with their grandchildren. Now I knew different. We certainly took our share and more. Those pictures today are so special and as I look at them I vividly recall to mind the personality plus of my favorite little girl.

MEDICAL TRIALS

During our years together, we had our share of surgeries and visits to the veterinarian. I'm not sure who it was the hardest on, Princess or me.

One afternoon when Princess was outside playing and I was inside working, I heard a shrill arrr...arrr...arr-rrrr. The crying, shrieking sound that I knew was Princess sent a cold chill piercing through my body as I ran to the sliding glass door. There I saw Princess trying to get up the flight of stairs from the lower deck to the upper deck in our backyard. I had no idea what was happening, but she was limping on three legs, holding one in the air, and I knew she was hurting. Once inside the house I couldn't see anything wrong but she continued holding up her right leg as though something was very wrong and looked at me as if to say, "Do something, Mom, please." I glanced at the clock, 5:30 p.m. I grabbed the telephone and punched out the vet's number, hoping he still would be in. "Bring her in right now," he said, and off we went. By the time we arrived at his office, she seemed to be okay. Upon examination, nothing. He asked us to come back the next morning for x-rays and indicated Princess would have to be anesthetized for the duration to get the x-rays he needed.

Saturday morning we headed off once again for the vet's office. I was told she would have to stay for a couple of hours to allow the anesthesia to wear off before I could take her home. A few hours later I returned to hear the diagnosis. Yes, she did have a problem. She was now sixteen months old and the anconeal bone in her elbow that should have fused with the ulna bone as she grew, didn't. Instead, this small bone piece was floating around and the shrieking the day before was caused from the pain when the bone piece had mislodged. "What does this mean?" I asked the vet. "Well, we really need to do surgery," he explained. The surgery would involve pinning the bone in place with the hope that it would then fuse. If it didn't, there was the possibility of amputation if it continued to cause problems later.

Understanding that there are always risks with surgery, I was naturally apprehensive, and leaving Princess at the vet's office the day of surgery was more than a little difficult. Her doctor called me as soon as he completed the surgery to say she had come through it just fine and that now we would begin the road to recovery and healing.

I was instructed to make a place for her at home where she could be confined for three weeks. A five by five foot area would do just fine, I was told. She was not to move around much and absolutely no stairs. Great, I thought to myself, we have a tri-level home with two flights of stairs. I couldn't possibly keep her couped up in a five by five area...the only area in the house that small was either the downstairs bathroom or the utility room. No way. Nor was I going to leave her alone. We had grown too close, we did everything together and we had been doing it for over a year.

Together we decided upon a solution that worked just fine, although it wasn't a five by five foot area. Princess and I camped out downstairs in the family room. The only problem was there was no bed and no sofa downstairs, only chairs, and I knew I could never sleep in them. I'd never been able to sleep sitting up. For three weeks an outside chaise lounge (one of the nylon web type) served as my bed. I wrapped myself in a blanket and dropped onto the chaise at bedtime. I'm sure Princess thought I looked more like a mummy than a mommy, but that was the best I could do without a sleeping bag. Princess slept on a three by five foot carpet piece, comfortably equipped with padding, during those three weeks. The only time I left her alone, other than while I was at work, was to take a shower and to fix meals. Even then I carried our meals downstairs and we dined together.

I don't know if it helped Princess, but it sure helped me. She had woven her way into the fabric of my heart, and I felt her pain as she endured the surgery and recovery period. Maybe it was then that I first really realized what it must be like to be a parent and have a child go through surgery. I couldn't have been more concerned. Fortunately, we never had any further problems associated with that surgery, but there would be others.

Another of her earlier surgeries was for the removal of a cyst located on the occipital bone, the protruding bone at the top of the skull between the ears. Surgery went fine, however this mother worried throughout the process as usual. Princess' hairstyle was distinctly altered for awhile as the vet gave her a sideways mohawk, removing all the hair on the top of her head between her ears. Ten days after surgery we returned to the vet for suture removal. Princess was a little trooper as he removed the stitches right there in the waiting room, however we would soon find out that suture removal was premature.

Later that Saturday afternoon, I was catnapping, lying prone on the living room sofa. When I woke up, I was both deeply touched and extremely frightened. Shock waves flashed through my body. There was Princess sitting patiently and looking at me as if to say, "I've been waiting for you to wake up, Mom, I need your help." And help she did need. There, right in front of my eyes, was the gaping wound where the sutures had been removed only hours earlier...the incision had reopened.

We had only been home a couple hours, but I knew the vet's office closed early on Saturday, so I called him at home. "Meet me at the office in thirty minutes," he said at the other end. So off to the office we went. It would be one of the last visits to that particular doctor. He was waiting when we arrived and immediately ushered Princess to the back for resuturing. Little did I know he hadn't planned on using any novocaine or similar anesthetic to numb the area needing sutures, but Princess endured the full procedure without so much as a whimper. When the vet returned to the waiting room with Princess and told me what he had done (or should I say, not done), I felt the pain all the way to my toes for Princess. And I knew I wouldn't be taking her back there again. Still to this day when I think about it I hurt for Princess because she was forced to experience that pain needlessly. But she never complained...not a single whimper or whine.

Another time when Princess was eight years and four months old she developed a myopian gland adenoma, a benign tumor, on the outside corner of her eyelid. She handled the surgery in her usual style (extremely well), but the real fun began when she arrived home. To keep Princess from scratching the sutures in her eyelid, she was required to wear an Elizabethan collar, more appropriately described as a lampshade or satellite dish. This strange looking object fit around her neck and extended out about twelve inches or so, just like a lampshade around the head. Naturally she couldn't see except for straight ahead and as she walked she bumped into walls and furniture because of her lack of peripheral vision. It was quite obvious she didn't like this foreign object at all and the madder she got the funnier she became. Defiance surfaced and could be seen all over her face! She was determined that if she had to wear that uncomfortable, cumbersome "helmet" everyone in the room would have to hear about it. If she missed hitting the doorjamb when she walked into a room she backed up, tried again and made sure she hit it with her second attempt. She wasn't satisfied until she had banged into the wall with her lampshade and made sure I knew she still had it on. It was really funny, but I did feel sorry for her. I couldn't imagine walking around with my peripheral vision cut off by some lampshade, let alone having to sleep in it...which she had to do every night for three weeks. As the wound healed, the itching began and it was an ordeal to keep her from scratching, in spite of the helmet. She couldn't get her paw to her face, but she did discover that if she put her head close to the corner of the sofa it would extend into the lampshade and allow her to scratch against the sofa arm. Princess was a real inventor when she needed something done!

I could go on and on about surgeries and visits to

the doctor, but it would be more of the same. We spent our share of time, and more, in preparation and recovery from surgeries. Princess and I weathered each medical storm together, as close as a parent and child could be, and we spent countless hours side by side during the recovery and healing processes. We really understood each other. I sensed her pain and I know she sensed my love and concern. Together we made it through all those trials.

THE TOUGH YEARS

Beginning a business with no capital, that is no savings whatsoever, probably isn't the wisest decision, but when I made the jump I made it big. No longer did I enjoy the luxury of a regular monthly paycheck and I had no other source of income...only what I could generate in my new business venture. I had been highly successful in insurance sales and insurance sales management, and when I decided to start my own sales, management and personal development training company on July 1, 1979, I thought success would come overnight. How wrong I was!

Princess was almost two and a half years old now. During those first years we had to be apart all day while I worked at my downtown Seattle office, but now was our opportunity to spend many more hours together as I worked out of our home.

The going wasn't easy. I borrowed from a bank and paid both household and business expenses from the loan for as long as it lasted. Without going into great detail, we had many months of very little income...compared to expenses, very little. There were times Princess and I laid in bed at night with our stomachs growling because we had nothing to eat. But I knew we'd make it, somehow. I just knew I had done the right thing.

I remember clearly the day the banker showed up at the front door telling me that since I was behind three months in house payments, and if I couldn't make a payment in the next few days, they would be forced to begin foreclosure proceedings. The very next day a tow truck showed up on our driveway and at the front door the driver made his appearance to repossess my new car. Fortunately it was in the garage and the garage was locked. I don't remember how I came up with the money to meet either of these obligations, but I did.

There would continue to be many days and months to follow when we would have a tough time paying the bills, but as the saying goes, when the going gets tough the tough get going. We wouldn't quit. It wasn't easy on me and somehow I knew it wasn't any easier for Princess. She seemed to sense the fear and frustration and stress I was experiencing. Many times she would come over by me and be close enough so she could touch me as if to say, "I'm here, we'll make it together." Through it all she was my best friend and constant companion. Many times out of the blue, when I was preoccupied with things and dealing with all the unresolved problems, she placed her front paws on my lap and reached up to my face with a big kiss. Or she would sit by me and lay her head in my lap. Her presence and her unconditional love and acceptance was often what kept me going. I had to make it not just for me, but for Princess. She was dependent upon me.

I came to think of Princess as my office manager. She was there with me as I went to work each day (since my office was in our home) and she was always well dressed...in a fur coat no less! Princess helped out in more concrete ways too. Often it was reflecting on our relationship that inspired me when I was writing material for the courses I developed and taught. For example, a necessary element in any successful communication is trust. And Princess exemplified this totally. Another is the willingness to listen...again, Princess always listened. Even if she didn't always obey, she did listen! And she knew what was said. She also knew much about encouragement and building self-esteem. Although my family loved me uncondi-tionally, Princess gave me an even deeper under-standing of unconditional love and acceptance. No matter how I looked, how I was feeling, how well I did or didn't do during a presentation, she never judged and was always there to love and accept me. Having her with me gave all the encouragement I needed. Perhaps it was her total devotion as well as her vitality and zest for life, that kept me going through the tough times. Whatever it was, we made it through them together.

HOUDINI

Princess knew that life was to be lived and evidently she didn't feel she could do much living caged in a kennel and being confined to a room when people were present in another.

During our years in Seattle, she had a very special kennel which served as her home away from home when I had to be out of town. On special occasions such as the first Christmas when I flew home to Mom and Dad's, she was served pheasant and stewing hens for Christmas dinner. The kennel owners, Bob and Pat, even sent Christmas cards addressed to Princess Kilbourn. They treated her more like their child than a boarder, and often took her out of the kennel to share some of their time and special attention in their home. Perhaps it was the first incident of Houdini that served as a catalyst for this nontraditional, exceptional treatment.

One day Bob and Pat were stirred by a rather rowdy commotion coming from the kennels. Dogs were wildly barking, seemingly bidding their presence. Upon inspection they discovered Princess happily and contentedly making her rounds, visiting each of the kenneled dogs as if to lend support and friendship to each. She had opened her own kennel gate and made her way down the long corridor connecting each kennel. She saw nothing unusual with her behavior and wasn't about to stop gaining her freedom and sharing her hospitality whenever she pleased. Much to her dismay, her kennel became the only one secured with a padlock!

Periodically, I was called out of town without much advance notice. One particular time her special kennel was completely full, and Princess couldn't stay with Bob and Pat. This time she stayed at her veterinarian's office, kenneled as usual, at least for a short while. Repeating the previous experience, her vet heard a commotion coming from the kennel area. Approaching the source of the noise, he found Princess had played Houdini. She had freed herself and was merrily making the rounds to meet her roomates. And once again, her kennel quickly gained the distinction as the only one with a padlock.

Princess' Houdini act wasn't confined to her regular kennel or the vet's office. She was just as masterful at home. It is one thing to push up the horseshoe shaped latch that closes a chain link gate and push it forward, but it is yet another when an animal pushes it up, then pulls the gate backwards to open the gate. Princess had been assigned the backyard duty one night as the downstairs recreation room (which contained her doggie door into her kennel) was being used for a meeting of the adult education committee of our church. That night, there were approximately thirty people all sitting around on the carpet downstairs, enjoying a glass of wine as we talked. It was literally wall to wall people, and wall to wall wine glasses as we discussed the education programs we would offer. Without a hint of notice, a sudden burst of energy in the shape of a German Shepherd filled the room.

Princess! Houdini again. She had opened the gate which separated her kennel from the rest of the backyard, entered the kennel and bounded through the doggie door to join the party unannounced.

On another occasion, the same group was meeting at our house for a home mass. Mass was held in the living room on the middle level of our house and Princess was kept downstairs so as not to interrupt Mass. I don't remember now what the homily was about, but I do remember Father Joe reflecting on a Peanuts cartoon. Precisely at the moment he repeated what Lucy had said in the cartoon, "Out damn dog," Princess opened the door at the bottom of the stairs, vaulted up the stairs and once again into the midst of our group. Mass or no mass, it was her house, and she wouldn't tolerate being separated from the action.

Princess loved to go in and out, much like a child. After multiple treks to the backyard one afternoon, I became impatient and told her she would have to stay inside for awhile, but she wasn't about to acknowledge my request. Walking away from her I heard the sliding glass door open. As I turned she was exiting through the door she had just opened. She had learned to open the door by pushing the handle with her nose...something she would continue to do whenever the door wasn't locked. The only real drawback was that she never learned to shut the door behind her!

Princess had a special way of making sure she was noticed. She had such a loving way about her that she crawled right into the hearts of people and took up residence. She loved people and she didn't want to be separated from them. And she made sure she wasn't, at least any more than necessary.

THE PROTECTOR

Of all her claims to fame, Princess couldn't possibly have gained the reputation for being a watchdog, although that really didn't make any difference to passersby on the street as they gazed at her through the window. Several police friends told me she would scare off people just by her presence and her bark.

Princess seemed to think our property line extended about as far as she could see, and when anyone was in sight she would bark. *She* knew she had lungs and vocal cords, *I* knew she had them, and *so did anyone else* within hearing range. I never have, to this day, really understood her thinking on this issue. She barked when I was at home, but friends told me that when I wasn't there and they dropped by to visit, Princess never barked at them. I never did figure out whether or not she barked at strangers when I wasn't there. Well, at least she barked when I was home and that made me feel pretty safe.

I remember one afternoon in July, 1981, shortly after we moved to Portland, Oregon, when the temperature soared to 104 degrees. Having lived in Seattle where 80 degrees was a hot day, the heat was unbearable for us, and we had no air conditioning in our new home. Wilted by the heat, I laid down on the sofa to take a nap. The model home sign had not yet been removed from the front lawn. Deep in sleep, I was awakened by an excruciating bark becoming more shrill with every warning attempt. As I awakened, I peered over the back of the sofa and discovered two unknown Oriental men standing in the foyer. Now I was ready to join Princess in the barking! They said, "This model home?" Startled, I said, "No, this not model home. What do you want, who are you?" Apologizing, they retreated quickly through the front door. I turned around to thank Princess for being such a good watchdog...but no Princess. Then I spotted her crouched between the wall and the freestanding fireplace...hiding! So much for the protection. She looked at me as if to say, "I did my part, the rest was up to you!"

There was one occasion when the tables were turned. I had forgotten to call Bob and Pat to tell them when I would be bringing Princess to the kennel. They had always asked to be notified so they could make sure their dogs could be put inside. Well, this time I didn't call. As I entered the gate with Princess, from out of nowhere a whole pack of dogs descended upon us. As they closed in, I was frightened they were going to hurt Princess, and I threw myself to the ground on top of Princess to protect her. Right at that moment, Bob and Pat emerged from their home and called off the dogs. Still shaking, Princess and I stood up, checked each other over to make sure we were okay and seeing that we were, proceeded on.

And so it continued. Princess loved people, almost everyone, but at least she barked when someone passed by or approached the house whenever I was there. I really did feel secure with her, even if she wasn't inclined to be a "guard" dog.

Fortunately, we never had to find out how she would have responded if there really had been an unwanted intruder.

MOMENTS OF LAUGHTER

Everyday was special with Princess, but there were those crazy, silly moments when laughter prevailed.

One day shortly after I began my business, while working in my office at home, I was interrupted by a strong nudge on my elbow. There she was, and the expression on her face was too quizzical to pass off lightly. I thought she simply wanted my attention, but reaching my hand down to pet her, Princess gently placed her jaws around my wrist. Now what? Tugging lightly as if to say, "Come," she persisted. I didn't seem to have much choice. "What do you want?" I asked her. Princess led me, of all places, into the bathroom and straight to the toilet where she promptly let go. And there was the cause for her concern. At the bottom of the toilet bowl laid her favorite latex toy...and she wasn't about to get it out for herself!

Another time I had decided that in order to be able to control Princess, she would have to learn discipline, and that meant obedience training. Checking out possible schools and training, we decided on private lessons to be given at our home. One particular day of training, it was very cold outside. Sue, her trainer, led Princess out to the sidewalk to practice, sit, stay and heel. As Sue stopped, Princess stopped, but there was no way she was going to sit on that cold concrete. So there she squatted, hind end about two inches from the ground! Cute, yes. Sue and I both laughed and Princess knew she had us. Of course, we knew laughing wouldn't help the training any, but it was such a sight that we couldn't control our laughter. There she stayed, squatted, as if to say, "I don't see you sitting on this cold concrete, and neither will I." There were so many times Sue would say to me, "She knows exactly what to do, but she is not going to do it...too wet, too cold, too whatever." Princess was indeed a strong-willed child!

Then there were the vitamins. I had been a believer in vitamins for years and my "child" was going to take them too. And she loved them, at least the chewable ones, but she disdained the non-chewable B complex. The chewables she quickly devoured and then begged for more. In fact, I had to take my vitamins first, or she begged for a second helping. But not so with the Bs. As she got a little older, I began giving her non-chewable vitamins because they were less expensive. That meant putting them in the back of her mouth and holding it shut until she swallowed. I don't know how she would do it, but when I thought she had swallowed them all (about ten at a time) and let go of her mouth, I turned my back and soon found the Bs on the floor. We went round and round with this one. Our neighbor, Terri, took care of Princess during her last year of life while I was on business trips. Princess was a defiant child when it came to taking her vitamins for Terri. As soon as Terri headed for the vitamins and said, "It's time for your vitamins," Princess headed for the far side of the dining room behind the table. And the chase began!

My house in Seattle was new when I bought it, and the fireplace was clean. I had lived there four and one-half months before Princess joined me, but I had yet to use the fireplace. Guess who did? For some strange reason, she loved crawling into the fireplace to rest. It was cute when she was little but years later, full grown, she still did it and it was just plain funny. Friends couldn't believe it when I told them. How could this full-grown German Shepherd fit? I just said, "Wait awhile and you'll see for yourself." Wait they did, and crawl into the fireplace Princess did. Fortunately, she kicked the habit immediately as soon as we began using the fireplace for its intended purpose.

Not many animals have their own private sun deck, but Princess enjoyed this rare privilege. I had a contractor build a doggie door so Princess could go outside whenever she pleased. The problem was getting back in because the drop to the ground outside was about two feet. One day, when Mom and Dad were visiting, Dad decided Princess needed a deck to walk out on, making it easier to exit and enter. A few hours later, Princess had her own private three foot deck covered with astro turf. Now she could get back inside the house without straining. Princess soon found another purpose besides exit and entry. She crawled out the doggie door, sat on her sundeck with her tail still inside the house under the doggie door flap, and wagged her tail whenever something tickled her fancy.

Princess had tremendous talent, and at times she seemed to have supernatural powers, but when it came to walking on water she fit more into the realm of the natural. One summer we drove down to Southern Oregon to visit Mom and Dad for a few days. Princess loved her Grandma and Grandpa, and she knew that's where we were headed as soon as we took the exit off the freeway leading to their house. As we pulled into the driveway, she exited from the car in her usual manner...after me, you're first! She ran to the front door and as soon as I opened it, she frantically sniffed and searched for a familiar grandparent. It didn't take her long. The back door was open and Dad was outside kneeling next to the swimming pool checking the water temperature. Suddenly, Princess found the open door and headed straight for the pool, as fast as her four legs would carry her. The problem was that she thought the solar pool covering was solid surface, and she failed to stop. Need I say more? Her walk on water routine failed, and the next thing I knew, Dad and I were drenched as we rescued Princess from the pool. Fortunately, she learned fast and that was the last time she tried to walk on water.

There were also delayed moments of laughter, delayed until the fear and panic passed. One afternoon I became acutely aware of how alone I was in an inordinately quiet house. I knew something was wrong, because it was never that quiet. I called and called for Princess, but I couldn't find her. I searched the house and still no Princess. The guest bedroom door was closed as it often was, so I hadn't thought to check there. Finally, a small voice inside me said, "Try the guest room," and sure enough, there she was, patiently waiting to be discovered. She had entered the room and somehow closed the door behind her. The bedroom floor was hardwood and whenever she tried to stand on her back legs she would slide. Maybe she had tried to open the door like she had done so many times before in other rooms, but in this room the slippery hardwood floors made it impossible. There she sat, quietly and patiently, waiting for Mom to find her.

Another of these moments of laughter was more mine than hers. One evening the delivery people arrived with the organ I had purchased and they were placing it in the space I had cleared. Princess was right in the middle trying to determine what this foreign object was doing in her home. That first night, as I began playing the organ, she retreated to the top of the stairs, as far away as she could get, yet still within viewing range, and sulked. Often I got up fifteen minutes early in the morning to play and she occupied the same place at the top of the stairs, resuming her sulking. It was her way of letting me know she disapproved of the unwelcomed intruder that captured the attention she felt should be hers. Whenever I played, she pouted. Another of her human traits emerged...jealousy.

Many times I couldn't help but laugh as I watched Princess eating, more like a human than a dog. No matter what I was eating, Princess wanted it too. Grapefruit, bananas, pickles, salad, vegetables, you name it, if I ate it, she at it too. She must have inherited her grandma's chocoholic addiction, however, because chocolate was one of her favorite treats. She loved chocolate chips, and M and Ms, and given one by one she would actually chew them as if to savor each morsel. One day, about an hour after we had together consumed an entire bag of chocolate chips, a newscast on television discussed the danger of feeding chocolate to dogs, because of an ingredient in chocolate that is actually poisonous to them. Fortunately, no problems were caused by our culinary delight that day, but I was very careful to limit Princess' chocolate treats from that day forward. Another of her favorites was popcorn, but *buttered only* thank you. She became very adept at picking out the buttered pieces and leaving the plain ones for me to pick up off her napkin. Princess also liked toast with peanut butter and jelly. Our routine was a bite for you and a bite for me. Afraid she might not get enough, she refused her first bite until I finally gave up trying to get her to take it and put it on the floor. Then she would stare at me as if to say, "Another, please." After she piled up three or four pieces, using the same routine, she finally ate. Just a safeguard, I guess, to make sure she got her fair share.

Princess had her own unique way of doing most things. She couldn't be content to eat her dinner where I placed the bowl. She invariably pawed at it until it was just where she wanted it, which often meant it ended up overturned on the floor. In an effort to be near me while I was working at the desk, laying alongside wasn't good enough. She always chose the spot under the desk where my legs were supposed to be. In the backyard of our home in Seattle, she loved to watch the neighboring snow white malamute who seldom did anything but sleep. Nevertheless, she spent hours in surveillance walking on the raised mound in our yard, determined not to miss any signs of life that the animal might exhibit. She didn't, however, walk on all four feet. Instead, she walked on her two back feet. I had never seen a dog do this, and I could hardly believe my eyes the first time I witnessed the event. She was able to take as many as six to eight steps before falling, then she walked again.

Throughout the years, I doubt that one day went by without Princess doing something that had me in hysterics. It has been said that laughter is the best medicine, and she was quite a pharmacist. She dispensed more "medicine" in one day than any pharmacist, I'm sure.

Mom and Dad, returning from a vacation one time, gave me a wall plaque they had picked up in one of their travels entitled, "What is a Little Girl?" It could have been meant for Princess rather than me. Either way, it fit. Here's the poem:

She is born into this world with an angel shine.
She gets a little older and worries you all the time.
She plays in the mud with your hat and your shoes,
And drags her doll...she has nothing to lose.
She uses the song of a bird, the stubbornness of a mule,
the antics of a monkey, curiosity of a cat,
slyness of a fox...
She musses and fusses and takes up your time.
She can cause more grief, happiness, dissatisfaction,
joy, embarrassment than anything else in your life.
But when your world falls apart and everything seems
a mess, she comes to you and says
I love you best...then you begin to see the
angel shine and realize you've loved her all the time.
                                        Author unknown

Princess did have an angel shine. She did worry me at times. Yes, she played in the mud and she did more than drag my doll. Her life was a song, she could be stubborn as a mule, her curiosity was bigger than any cat's, and she could be as sly as a fox. But she was always there to comfort, to love and encourage laughter. And through it all, I loved her immensely.

NOW I LAY ME DOWN TO SLEEP

From the time she was a baby, with the exception of the first few weeks when she spent nights in the garage, Princess took up nighttime residence on our waterbed next to me. Sure, it was cute and I loved her company, but I guess I forgot that German Shepherds do grow up! Nevertheless, up until her very last day, I had a sixty-four pound German Shepherd sleeping with me.

If only children were that easy to get to bed! When Princess was tired, she crawled into bed on her own, she knew it was bedtime, and headed for the bedroom. I remember several nights, however, when I stayed up writing into the wee hours of the morning, that Princess wandered down the hall, sat in front of the bedroom door and yelped, "Mom, it's time for bed."

My routine for years had been to read for thirty minutes or so at bedtime. I had done this for years, and I saw no reason to change just because I had a new companion. If I read too long without paying attention to her, Princess would lay her head in my lap. That lasted for a few short minutes. If that wasn't enough to capture my attention, I soon found a cold, wet nose under the book pushing its way toward me. She always had to make sure I knew she was there. Sometimes when I stayed up late Princess would nap while I wrote, and when I was ready for bed she was ready for play. It took many pillow fights and wrestling matches on the bed to exhaust her energy enough to calm her down and prepare her for sleep.

I know to some people this would seem ridiculous, but those of you who love animals will understand. That cuddly ball of fur was a delight to feel. I often put my arm around her and quietly we drifted off to sleep. During my earlier days of living alone I slept rather lightly, but now with Princess I slept much more soundly. Although she was never what you could call a guard dog, I knew she would let me know if anything unusual was going on outside and I felt very secure.

One of my very favorite moments of the day was waking up in the morning. When Princess was little it was a bit different as she continually woke me up when she thought we had enough sleep, not realizing there were times when sleeping-in *was* appropriate. As she got a little older, she settled down and stayed down until I woke up, and those waking moments were very special. So often I'd wake up facing her side of the bed and laying there on her pillow facing me were two big ears, a big nose, and two beautiful big brown eyes staring as if to say, "Good morning, Mom, you're finally awake! I still miss that morning wake up.

Princess was very much like me. As the years passed she became a night person rather than a morning person. I would get up each morning and take a shower, dry my hair, style it, put on my make-up, and she would stay on the bed napping. She knew the routine well, and as soon as I walked out of the bathroom, she would get up off the bed and head for the kitchen, ready for breakfast.

Bedtime has always been a special part of my day...a time for quiet and reflection, prayer and meditation; time to release all the events and activities of the day and prepare for a good night's sleep. It was such a joy to share those moments with Princess and to wake up to her sparkling eyes each morning. Those are still some of my toughest moments today as I experience them alone without Princess beside me.

BEYOND HUMAN PERCEPTION: THE CANINE TEACHER

Many people look at an animal and believe that what you see is what you get. As each day passed and our years together unfolded, I sensed in Princess an incredible awareness and understanding of her surroundings and events...indeed an acute *awareness of life*. She lived fully in the here and now, squeezing all the pleasure and meaning she could get from each moment, a lesson we humans often need to learn. She was *totally alive.*

The first time she saw snow was when we had an unusual eight inches in Seattle. The yard a winter wonderland, her curiosity was piqued. Legs disappearing as she took her first snow walk, she was completely entranced and amused by this uncommon white. Princess would romp in the snow, then stop to sniff it as though she was contemplating its origin. When she was called inside she would lie with her nose poking between the drapes, gazing out into the yard through the glass doors like she was watching to make sure it didn't get away before she could experience it again. She was so aware, so alive, and really took in all that made up her environment.

Princess had quite a vocabulary, but one of her favorite words was "walk." As soon as I said, "Do you want to go for a walk?" she ran to her leash and back to me, back and forth until I got up to put it on her. At other times she wouldn't wait, she dragged the leash to me. Walks with Princess were wonderful learning experiences and sensitivity awareness sessions. No hurry for her, she wanted to stop all along the way to explore. She loved the smell of flowers and would hesitate long enough to satisfy her senses with each unique fragrance before moving on. The first daffodils of the year were her favorite, I think. Thoroughly enchanted, she tarried long enough to examine them deliberately. The first flower arrangement she saw, a spray of roses and carnations, was sent to our house by one of my insurance agents commemorating my four-year anniversary with the company. Princess was fascinated by the display and smelled each flower in turn after they arrived, periodically returning during the day to repeat the process. Perhaps she received more enjoyment from them than I did. Watching Princess in her unhurried encounter with life really taught me the meaning of stopping to smell the roses.

Toys were a frequent part of her playtime, and she entertained herself very well during those many hours I spent writing and reading. Among her toys was a heavy rubber ball the size of a tennis ball. Two flights of stairs in our house served as part of her playground, and standing at the top she rolled the ball down the stairs, retrieved it, and repeated the procedure. Another favorite was dropping the ball on the uncarpeted kitchen floor, watching it bounce and gleefully bounding after it. She seemed to love the sound it made as it hit the floor and the fun of retrieving it, wondering where it would land next. I think I now know how a parent feels when their child is given a toy drum set by a well-meaning relative or friend. It didn't take long to decide that a tennis ball would be much more suitable for in-house play, and a lot quieter, still serving the same purpose. Nevertheless, she loved to make noise and learned that she could create a special kind of noise with her toenails as she pranced around the kitchen floor, which she did frequently, delighted to hear her version of tap dancing. As I watched her playing, even when I was busy and couldn't join in the fun, I became more aware of how important it is to be happy no matter what the circumstances, even when you don't get your way. Princess preferred that I play with her, but it wasn't always possible. There was work to be done. Even so, she seemed to understand that happiness isn't a station you arrive at, nor was it based upon always getting what you want, rather it was how you made the journey with what you had. Whatever the circumstances were, she made the best of them always enjoying her life, day by day, moment by moment. Another lesson from my canine teacher.

Nothing went unnoticed by Princess unlike humans who often proceed through life without taking the time to enjoy all there is to see and experience in their surroundings. The littlest bugs and spiders fascinated her. When she spotted one she curiously trailed it to see where it would go and what it would do. Her curiosity of bees, however, got the best of her and resulted in minor surgery as I pulled the stinger from her nose. Another exploration that frequently concluded with a quiet, quick retreat were the visits over the fence by neighboring cats. They just weren't open to developing a relationship, no matter how hard Princess tried, much as in the world of human relationships. Nevertheless, Princess lived her life with an expectant spirit of discovery, always open to new growth and seldom afraid to risk.

Of the many lessons to be learned in life, one she lived by and taught me well was to live life in the present...to enjoy each moment as it is given to us. She understood that life, in its fullest sense, doesn't begin in the future. I learned from her that living in the present means being alive and fully involved in the life you are living at the moment...to be present to what you are doing at the time. She taught me to "tune in" to whatever I am doing.

Perhaps the very most important lesson she taught was unconditional love and forgiveness. There were no "ifs," no strings attached. She didn't care if I was well-dressed, had my make-up on or hair combed. She didn't judge and she held no grudges. Even when she was disciplined, she always returned to my side with a look that said, "I love you anyway, Mom."

Princess had such intelligence, in a very real way it seemed more like wisdom. She widened the dimensions of my life and intensified my participation and awareness of living. At times I pondered whether or not she just might be more advanced that I, a human, when it came to the essence of living.

FIRST FEARS

"No, I didn't see what I thought I saw," I calmly told myself as Princess climbed off the couch, legs wobbling unsteadily. "She's just not totally awake, and besides, she's had quite a day of long walks," I tried to convince myself. That was the first sign of what was to develop over the next sixteen months.

Carefully I continued watching Princess as she walked about, trying to relieve my concern that anything was wrong. But as the next few months passed, I couldn't deny there was something unusual, something I couldn't pass off as over-exertion or sleepiness.

Our next visit to her veterinarian confirmed the fact that something abnormal was occurring, but what we didn't know. Pulling into the driveway of her doctor's office, Princess became restless. She had visited this place many times and certainly didn't associate that building with fun. I told her it was okay and that she didn't have to stay there...we were just going for a check-up. In her almost human way, she seemed to acknowledge what I was telling her and her trembling stopped as her uneasiness faded. Fortunately, we had an excellent veterinarian. Dave was always empathetic and extremely compassionate. He graciously offered whatever time it took to talk with Princess and calm her fears...and additional time to ease my fears and listen to my concerns. Certainly there must have been times he felt he was dealing with an overprotective, oversensitive mother. If he did, he never let on.

No diagnosis was made, except that it wasn't hip dysplasia. Her recent x-rays showed no signs of this relatively common disorder. The possibility was a disc problem, for which surgery might be indicated, or the other possibility, spinal myelopathy, for which there was no cure and no treatment. Princess was prescribed an anti-inflammatory medication to see if that would help. If it did, there was a good chance it was a disc problem and surgery might correct the problem.

I tried to talk myself into believing the medication was helping, but she seemed to have no pain, not indicative of a disc. Approximately four months after the first signs, Dave explained spinal myelopathy as a degeneration of the myelin sheath around the spinal cord. This meant, if this was what she had, that she would eventually lose control of her legs. His associate examined Princess and also felt it was not a disc, probably spinal myelopathy. They both suggested we see a specialist, a neurosurgeon, to confirm the diagnosis, but since there wasn't anything that could be done anyway, we prolonged the visit to the specialist, not wanting to face the horrible reality.

By now, Princess was unable to crawl up on the waterbed with me at night; her back legs had weakened and just wouldn't make it. It was then that we began our year of sleeping on the hideabed in the third bedroom. Even the regular bed in the guest room was too high. As the days and months passed, Princess' unstable condition worsened until she could no longer even make it up onto the hideabed without my help.

About that time Mom and Dad were in Portland visiting us again. Watching the little girl they had come to love caused them much pain as the reality hit that she wouldn't be with us forever. Sure we knew she wouldn't live forever. But this...this was too soon. She was only eight and a half years old. Her grandfather lovingly spent a few hours in the garage building her a three foot by three foot by eight inch box to be used as an extra step to help Princess get onto the bed. She used this for about six months, until even that step was too much. When this no longer worked, I lifted her back legs and helped her onto the bed each night.

Fortunately, the spinal myelopathy had not affected her front legs; they were still strong and stable so it was only necessary to raise her back legs much like the wheelbarrow game I played when I was young. I remember how Mom and Dad, or even my younger brother, would pick up my back legs, me walking on my hands, calling me a "wheelbarrow." Only now this wasn't fun. It only reminded me of the inevitable. *How much longer did we have? What was going to happen?*

"Cheryl, I'd like to perform a myelogram on Princess," the neurosurgeon said. "It will tell us whether or not she has a disc problem. If that is ruled out, and if there are no signs of tumors present, my diagnosis will confirm the spinal myelopathy."

We scheduled the myelogram and Princess once again visited the neurosurgeon. We always talked about these things before they happened, and she never complained. She was required to stay overnight during the myelogram procedure and the next twenty-four hours without her seemed like a week. I missed her presence at home, I worried about her condition and I was plagued by the realization that too soon I might possibly be spending all my nights without Princess. That night I prayed the neurosurgeon would find the problem was with a disc.

As painful and uncomfortable as the myelogram was, Princess was a real trooper and as the doctor brought her in to me, she showed no signs of pain, just excitement to see her mom. As we sat together in the exam room we listened to the doctor as he gave us the results and spoke the dreaded words... "No, Cheryl, there is no evidence of a disc problem, and there is no tumor observable. My diagnosis is spinal myelopathy." *Spinal myelopathy...spinal myelopathy...spinal myelopathy.* Those words reverberated in my head like the incessant haunting of a nightmare. At once I felt like I was in quicksand and there was nothing I could do. Two words that I didn't want to hear. Two words that meant so much hurt ahead. Two words that meant the beginning of the end. I was soon to discover the intense pain of loss that begins long before the end.

As he explained the prognosis, the neurosurgeon told me we probably had eight months at best. That was the norm after diagnosis. He went on to explain that she would lose control of her legs and probably with that she would lose control of her bladder and bowels. I just couldn't believe it was happening. Not to Princess. Not now. Not ever.

In my mind, I was reliving the fact that she had had symptoms for nine months already...*did we really have eight more months?* So many questions, so little time. And so many prayers. Please, God, please let a miracle happen. Please let Princess recover from this. Please let her live. I can't imagine living without her. She's been my life for almost nine years now. She's my best friend. Please, God, please.

Those were to be my words every night for the next seven months.

THE DAYS TO FOLLOW

Although every day with Princess was special, now each day held new meaning. We spent more time just being together. When friends wanted to get together for dinner, we almost always had dinner at my house so I wouldn't have to be away from Princess. I found myself going home immediately after teaching a class or seminar or giving a speech so I could be with her.

Princess and I spent hours talking. I told her over and over how much I loved her, and in her special way, she did the same. I seldom watched television, but when I did, Princess was right there by my side and if there were animals in the show, even she would watch. Throughout our years together whenever an animal was hurt or died on a television program, I always hugged Princess as if I was protecting her, letting her know I wouldn't let it happen to her. But now the scene changed. I put my arms around her and tears trickled down my face, knowing this was beyond my control and soon I would experience a very great loss. In her own distinctive way she seemed to be trying to console me with kisses and cuddling, reminding me to enjoy every moment we shared. Those kisses were so special; they always had been. Princess was a great one for showing her affection.

Although it became difficult for Princess to get around, for awhile at least, she could still make her way to the car. I helped her and we headed for a park, or a country stream, anywhere, just somewhere to be alone together in a quiet, rural setting. And again we would talk.

The doctors told me there was no known cause for spinal myelopathy, but I racked my brain to come up with a reason. It never came. We had been so careful. She had all her shots on schedule, regular check-ups, she was fed the best of diet and plenty of vitamins. None of that eased my guilt now. I felt there must have been something I could have done to prevent this from happening. But there were to be no answers; only more questions.

The last few months were difficult. I'm not even sure I can explain the depth of pain that was becoming my daily uninvited visitor...the pain that soon became a constant intruder that wouldn't leave. I couldn't picture myself without Princess and I couldn't picture her without me. I recall several weekends when I cried uncontrollably for hours, knowing the inevitable was approaching. Many days I would sit and hold her, crying until I felt there couldn't possibly be any tears left, knowing we would have to say good-bye. I knew when I got her that if I lived a normal life I would outlive her, but the good-bye was coming sooner than I expected. I had done everything I could to keep her healthy. *Why wasn't that enough? Why this? Why now? Why Princess?* The pain was so great...at times so great that no amount of anything could stop the tears. I had expected at least thirteen or fourteen years with her, and it looked like we would barely make nine. Did we have the eight months the neurosurgeon suggested?

During that time Princess tried to comfort me. She really seemed to understand the hurt I was feeling. She knew I needed her right by my side and there she stayed. The days came and went and the 1985 holidays were approaching. I knew they would be difficult, happy and sad at the same time, realizing this would be our last Thanksgiving, last Christmas, last New Year and last birthday on this earth. With each holiday the pain became more intense and although we enjoyed each other fully, the reality still loomed like a dark cloud over our lives.

A few days before Christmas, Princess and I drove to Southern Oregon to be with Mom and Dad, and my brother and his family. By this time, her condition had greatly deteriorated, making it difficult for her to rest comfortably in the back seat of the car. To ease her discomfort, we used boxes and covers for padding to extend her bed area into what would normally be the passengers' leg room, giving her more room to lie how ever she could be most comfortable. Somehow I knew this would be our last long trip together, and I wanted to make it comfortable and memorable for her...and for me.

Christmas morning Princess was just as excited as all the rest of us. My niece and nephew, Krystal and Brian (twins, then age two) and Charlie (then age seven) were dancing with delight and with children's incredible anticipation as Grandpa distributed all the Christmas presents in our family's traditional style. Mark and Karen, my brother and sister-in-law, had a springer spaniel, Bogie, who also shared the day. Not to be forgotten, there were presents for Princess and Bogard as Grandpa presented their gifts, they jumped right in with the rest of us and tore open their packages.

One gift from "Mom" was a hard, nylon dog bone that Princess loved. Somehow I think those are supposed to be indestructible, but Princess managed to chew them down and replacement was always in order for birthdays and other giving occasions. No sooner had Princess opened this gift when cousin Bogie felt it was better suited for outdoor use. And that was the last of Christmas present number one. To this day we know that somewhere in Mom and Dad's backyard is Princess' new, unused bone, buried for safe keeping.

Later that day Princess shared in the Christmas dinner with turkey and all the trimmings. We all did everything we could to make sure it was a special Christmas for her and one we would all remember.

COMMUNICATING: HEART AND SOUL

As the new year began and the days pressed on, bedtime and our nightly ritual of reading and talking became ever more intense. I was acutely aware of our numbered days together and I wanted to spend as much quality time as I could being close, just being together.

Many nights as I read, Princess would lie next to me staring into the air as if in deep thought. But one night something was different. It was late and as usual we were in bed (the hideabed) and I was reading. Comfortably, Princess laid next to me with her gaze focused on a point that seemed to extend far beyond the confines of the room. Perhaps I would not have been so aware, but I had been spending a great amount of time in meditation and I had been reading some books on auras and astral travel. Was Princess tuned in...was she "out there somewhere?"

Princess was staring far off into some unknown territory beyond what my senses could identify. Something had her attention and was holding it firmly, contentedly. Not only could I see that was true, but it filled the air and couldn't go unnoticed. I sat there quietly watching her and questions filled my mind. *What was she thinking? Was she contemplating where she would be?* As I listened intuitively I became aware that Princess' identity was, in fact, far beyond her physical body.

Although she was a dog, she was most certainly an intelligent, thinking being. I had seen this many times as she went about her daily activities.

This occurrence was in her last couple months of earthly life. *Was she contemplating the hereafter? Did she know? Did she have insight into the great beyond...beyond her physical existence?* I focused on Princess for about half an hour, quietly watching and searching for every clue, listening for any revelation. And then Princess turned toward me, her eyes connecting with mine as if she saw into and beyond me. *And I knew she was silently communicating with me.* The understanding was due in part to my willingness to go beyond her animalness, to be open to the humility I always felt in her presence and to the unexplored part of myself that was becoming more real. It was at this moment we communicated in a way we humans say *"with the heart."* A kind of speech that needs no words, no sounds, no verbal utterances. I knew we had spoken the same language, that we were *at one in mind and heart.*

In the months that followed, Princess and I maintained that special communication like a cord that binds together. I learned from her how to let go of human superiority and let the special bond express itself through and between us. Call it God, Universal Mind or Superior Consciousness, whatever. We had become "at one." We were experiencing total companionship and communication that blossomed and flourished in a mutual atmosphere of respect, trust, love, admiration and loyalty.

Just as when two people communicate on the same plane and find they need no words to really hear the other or understand, yet at the same time are totally in tune, Princess and I had connected in a most beautiful, deeply moving way. We seemed to be in total harmony, perfect accord. I had come to really know and understand that we were both living expressions of the same God. We had crossed the boundary of humanness and dogness and found that indeed, *no boundaries exist unless we place them there in our own minds.*

I became more aware of the times when Princess would be sleeping in one room while I was writing or doing something in another room and my thoughts would turn to her. In an instant she appeared as if I had called her name out loud, responding to my mental call. I didn't have to be within the visual range for her to know what I was thinking. Many people had commented on this through the years, including the eleven year old neighbor boy who said, "I've never seen a person so involved with another person with hair all over their body like you and Princess. You read each others minds." At other times, I would be sitting quietly reading in the living room and Princess would be asleep, or so I thought. As I watched her, mentally talking with her, often she would wake up, lift her head, gaze at me, and then walk over and sit at my feet as if to say, "Let's talk." Princess had a special way of cocking her head to one side, then the other, moving her ears carefully as if to be sure and catch all I was saying. That's what I miss most today, her companionship, her knowing, her communicating with me in a manner that goes beyond mere words...her complete understanding of my feelings.

EARLY GRIEVING

The grieving process began with the diagnosis in September and continued throughout the coming months, but it isn't quite the same as the reality of making the decision. I discussed with Dave on many occasions how I would know it was time, since this wasn't a condition that would mean a natural death. There would come a time when I would have to face the reality and make the decision myself. Over and over Dave would tell me, *"Cheryl, you will know. I just know in my heart that you'll know when it is time."*

I'll never forget the day. It was Monday, April 14. I had prayed, I had talked with Princess and now I felt as though the time had come. I watched her deteriorate day by day, unable to walk except by scooting on the floor carrying her bodily weight with her front legs...and I felt so helpless. I've never dreaded making a telephone call so much in my entire life and I'm not sure now how I ever managed to dial Dave's number. The hardest part of the decision was that I had to make it. Oh, how I wanted to let Princess make the decision, but in the end I knew I had to make it myself. It just wasn't fair. *Why should I have to be the one to make this decision about her life? What if it really wasn't time? What if?* My mind was fuzzy and confused. I didn't want the responsibility of choosing for her,

47

yet it still kept coming back to me. Making the decision and calling Dave was undoubtedly the hardest thing I've ever had to do. But in my heart, I felt the time was now.

Since Dave and I had discussed this at length on several occasions we already knew that the euthanasia would be completed at Princess' and my home. I couldn't bring myself to take her to a place where she began trembling and shaking the moment we drove into the driveway, nor could I stand the thought of leaving her in a sterile, medical environment. I kept visualizing Princess being lifted onto a cold, stainless steel table and that just wasn't right. At least not for us.

Because she was a family member, because we had grown so close, I knew that I wanted to be with her to the end. I knew I'd never be able to abandon any of my family members or friends during their final moments of life on this earth and I wouldn't abandon Princess. No matter how difficult it might be I would see her through...I would be right there by her side.

As I spoke with Dave and we checked both our schedules, it was decided that we couldn't schedule the euthanasia until Thursday. So on Monday, April 14, we both marked our calendars...*Thursday, April 17, 4:45 p.m.*

Unless you have experienced this yourself, you will never know what those last days meant to us. In so many ways it was very painful, knowing we had only three nights, then two nights, then one more night together. Every night I was acutely aware of the hours silently slipping away. Not one of those nights passed that I didn't hold her, sleeping with her right close by and crying until I thought I could cry no more. But there was also a very special beauty to those nights. Unlike so many people who never have the chance to say goodbye when passing from this life comes so unexpectedly, we had glorious hours of conversation and total communication. We were able to say all we wanted to say and share all those special moments that were just between us; moments that time will never erase. Some memories fade with time, but the memories of those last few days are as vivid today as the days they were made.

Although the decision was made, I wavered during the next few days. When I arrived home from a speaking engagement or training session Princess would be waiting at the door. Obviously, unable to walk by this time, it was a major effort to pull herself on her hind end with her front legs to get to the door, but she never failed to greet me. And she was just as excited to see me then as she was when she could greet me by jumping and putting her paws on my shoulders and her tongue across my face to welcome me home as she had done for so many years.

Each time she met me my mind flashed...*is it really time?* Maybe I should call Dave back. Maybe a little while longer. I continued praying for wisdom and discernment...for knowledge and guidance. And I kept hearing, *"Don't destroy Princess' dignity, she has feelings too. You love her and because you love her, let her go home now and be at peace."*

FINAL HOURS

Thursday, April 17. The alarm clock sounded at 4:00 a.m. It would be a long, difficult, painful day. I had wished my schedule was clear of any commitments that day, but I had two training sessions to conduct. The first at 6:00 a.m. Before rising, I talked with Princess for awhile and told her I had to give a talk, but I'd be home as soon as I could. As I showered and dressed, getting ready for work, Princess laid in bed as was customary waiting for me to finish. My mind was overflowing with hundreds of thoughts skipping from the business activities of the day and back to Princess. So many details of our life together flashed through my mind and I knew 4:45 would be here all too soon. As I left the house at 5:30, I hugged Princess and told her I would be back soon.

The night before, our last night together, I fervently prayed, *"Please, God, please give me a sign that this is right, that I made the right decision."* As I arrived home at 9:30 after the training session, Princess was waiting in the living room, unable to meet me at the door for the first time ever. I felt like I was being torn to shreds inside...only seven more hours. As I entered the living room, there was my sign. And I knew, really knew, this was the time. There on the carpet was a black stool, black as charcoal, and I knew it meant

50

internal bleeding. Yes, the disease was causing malfunction internally, no longer only affecting her legs. As much as it hurt to see this, I knew it was the answer to my prayer. Again, for two hours Princess and I sat quietly and talked before I had to leave again.

The next class was normally from 1:00 to 4:00 p.m., but on Tuesday I had asked the participants if we could meet one hour earlier on Thursday, so I would have a little time to spend with Princess before Dave arrived. Understanding, they agreed, so I left at 11:30 for the class. I'm not sure how I got through either of the training sessions that day, but there was so much support extended by the participants that really helped. We concluded class at 3:00, and I hurried home to share the final hours, alone with Princess.

From 3:15 until 4:35, I sat with Princess on the floor, my arms around her as we said our private goodbyes. We communicated at a level that once again transcended her animalness and brought us together as equals as we had done so many times before. She seemed to know the immediacy of the situation. I felt sure she was aware. We thanked each other for the beautiful years that no one could ever take from us. We expressed our love and we cried softly. I believe there were tears in her eyes, too, as our eyes and our hearts joined lovingly.

At 4:35 Connie arrived, a girlfriend who had lost her seventeen year old son in an automobile accident just three months before. I had been with Connie through her tragic loss, and now she was there to support me as I faced what I feared to be the most terrible moment I would ever have to experience. During the last few moments the florist arrived with a beautiful flowering plant for me and for Princess. Within the next few minutes a friend brought another flower arrangement by. Then Connie took the last pictures of Princess and I as we together stared at the camera trying to muster up a smile.

And then the doorbell rang. It was 4:45.

LAST MOMENTS

"Hello, Dave," I said as he entered our home, accompanied by his assistant. We sat in the living room and Dave shared with me what he would do and the possible reactions. He indicated there was a possibility that Princess would make a final gasp for air, or that she would involuntarily urinate or deficate, and that there might be some involuntary twitching after the euthanasia. He caringly prepared me so I wouldn't be frightened or upset if any of these occurred. We talked for about fifteen minutes, then he said, "Are you ready?" *It was really happening.*

By now I had a profound sense of peacefulness. I was ready to do what I felt was best for Princess, no matter how much it hurt me. I really believed she would go on living and now I wanted to make her journey into the land beyond a good one.

Dave helped me get Princess into the bedroom and onto the hideabed where we spent the nights together for the past year. As we put Princess on the bed she became frightened and tried to get down. I spoke to her softly and said it was okay, and with that she relaxed and quieted herself. I'll never forget those last few moments. Princess became very peaceful and looked into my eyes with a look that could only be interpreted as, *"Mom, I love you and I trust you. Do what needs to be done."* I can still see her face today as I recall those final moments. Although Dave, his associate and Connie were in the room with us, Princess never once took her beautiful eyes from mine, eyes that were loving, giving...and knowing. We talked softly and I held my arms around her neck as Dave prepared the injection. Once again, we expressed our love for each other as we said our goodbyes, as though no one was in the room but the two of us.

Without any fighting, Princess quietly accepted the injection, still looking at me, eyes penetrating my soul...totally loving, totally trusting. As the sodium pentathol began to take effect, which took a couple minutes, Princess became drowsy, and then she laid her head gently and softly along my arm and transcended this life.

When Dave was sure she no longer had a heartbeat, that she was "asleep" to this life, we sat together talking softly. No tears, no more hurting for Princess, just peace at that moment. Communicating nonverbally, Dave knew I needed to hold her for a few minutes and he just let us be, together for the last time.

Before Dave left, he shared a few words with me that were so special; words I will always remember and hold close to my heart. He said, "Cheryl, the bond was so strong between you and Princess, so beautiful...and it was expressed in these final moments so clearly. You know, Cheryl, as a veterinarian I don't often get to experience this kind of demonstration of love that I just witnessed. It is really very special."

Then Dave left, taking Princess in a blanket, to have her body cremated and return her ashes to me.

LONELY NIGHTS AND PAINFUL MORNINGS

As Dave left with Princess, with her physical body, *I knew deep inside* that Princess' spirit was still alive. I would miss her, yet I believed I would feel her presence, really feel her presence, many times in the days ahead.

I was fortunate to have friends who stood by me through the transition. That first evening, Connie stayed for several hours and we talked and talked. We discussed the loss of her son and the loss of my Princess. We remembered the new year's party I had had two years before with both her son and Princess there. We recalled the walks her son shared with Princess and the many, many summer evenings that Connie, Princess and I strolled through the neighborhood. I got out my pictures and we laughed...and cried...remembering the numerous moments of pleasure and frolic and hurt.

The first evening several friends cared enough to

be there for me. When Connie left that evening, Roxanne came to spend the night, not wanting me to be alone. Delores came by to see if she could help in any way, just to make sure I was okay. And Jan called to say she was praying for me. It was so special, so meaningful, even though they couldn't take away the pain, to know they understood that Princess was more than "just a dog" to me. They really understood our bond and the void that was now a part of me. My family called me that night too, as well as other friends. They knew how much I loved Princess and how much I was hurting. It helped to know they cared and it did make a difference.

Sleep didn't come easily that night. Although I was exhausted from the emotional drain and the piercing emptiness I was feeling, all I wanted to do was talk about Princess and look at all our pictures. Roxanne and I talked for hours before retiring, as I relived so many special moments that Princess and I shared. Although during our years together there were nights when we were apart while Princess was at the vet's or in a kennel until I could pick her up the next day, that was my first night *really* alone without Princess. The pain of her absence already penetrated the depths of my being. I don't remember falling asleep, but then...

Friday morning. And now, a world without Princess. Going to bed without her was just not the same, nor was waking up in the morning without her.

I missed her immensely. The pain of loss, of emptiness, was so intense I felt it would never end. The question I kept asking myself was, "Will I ever get over this pain, or will it torment me the rest of

MORNING...
 We wake and cuddle,
 talking to each other about
 the day ahead.
Off to work,
 be productive.
Evening walks together,
 eating popcorn,
 watching movies,
 romping and playing.
Nightly reading,
 quiet gazes,
 in tune,
 together.
Now she's gone.
Night again.
 Not again.
 Not without Princess.
 Dear God, no.
 Not now, not ever.
MOURNING.

my life?" No answers, only more questions. Selfishly I wanted her back. I had loved her as my child and my best friend for over nine years. She was a totally dedicated companion. Her entire life was devoted to me...helping, loving and protecting. It was as though she had reached perfection in unconditional loving, always putting me before herself.

The vascillation between hopeful recovery and preparing for death was emotionally exhausting and now I would begin the process of working through the grief and pain. It was as though I had to learn how to be a single person again, to learn all over how to be happy and fulfilled, alone. I had to keep reminding myself that Princess was no longer in pain, that now she would no longer suffer from that terrible degeneration and limitation caused by her physical illness. But even that wasn't enough to terminate the indescribable, gut wrenching feeling. I would live with it for months to come.

It seemed as if everything I did and everywhere I turned I was reminded of all our special moments together. I felt like my insides were being stripped from within me, and I was moving in slow motion. Now there was no Princess to wake up to. No Princess to share meals with me. No Princess waiting, peering through the drapes as I returned home each day. No Princess to interrupt my nightly reading with a gentle nudge of her cold, wet nose. *Emptiness*...that's all there was left...and a hole in my heart big enough to walk through.

GOING HOME

Many people have since said to me that they could never do what I did, that is to be there when their pet was euthanized. But to me it was a most beautiful experience and gave witness to our bond of love, our becoming family. Let me explain the best I can.

The outcome was inevitable. Princess had to be euthanized and that was a fact, but I had the choice as to how to go about it and a veternarian that was willing to help us in any way. Because Princess was more than an animal to me, because she was indeed a family member, I knew there was no way I could take her to Dave's office, leave her, desert her and not be with her because of my own pain. When it was over, I realized that it was really much easier to go through it together, just as I would with any of my family and my friends. Being there with her to the end was so meaningful...moments I will always cherish. Princess *knew*, and it seemed as if she was trying to make it easier for me.

Something wonderfully strange, but very real, happened at the moment there was no further life in her body. Something glorious, something beautiful that I had not anticipated. I KNEW there had been no death. I know today, without a doubt in my mind and heart, that Princess did not die. She was, at that instant, transformed and continues to live. I could feel it to the very core of my being and to this day I truly believe her spirit lives on. Perhaps some people feel that only the human spirit lives on, but inside I know differently. I know my Princess still lives and I have never wavered in that belief. The stained glass window I made of a butterfly and three flowers (with Princess' inquisitive help) is a reminder today of the fact that she still lives. Just as a caterpillar dies to the old life and is transformed into a free, beautiful butterfly, so too, Princess has been transformed and is now living without the bondage of her physical body.

My decision to cremate Princess was only to be a reminder to me. A reminder that I do have the physical body of Princess, but the real Princess still lives on. It was a decision I have never regretted. Today, her ashes remain with me and are a constant reminder of this.

RETURN VISITS

The moment of transformation, Princess' passing from this life, was a profoundly peaceful transition. Within the first few hours, in spite of the emptiness, I felt a tremendous sense of knowing that she would return. I didn't know how and I didn't know what I would experience at those moments.

Princess first returned one afternoon when I was home. I felt her presence intensely and as I moved from room to room Princess was with me. I couldn't see her and I couldn't touch her, but for several hours I knew she was there. It was then that I had my first real vision of Princess that would recur again and again for the months to follow. Although she no longer lived in her physical body, the vision was of her running and playing, tongue wagging from the playful exertion, free from the limitations of her physical disease. I kept seeing her look back at me to be sure I was watching saying, "Mom, see, I can jump and play...I'm okay...please don't be sad."

On another occasion I had returned home one evening just as a storm began wildly dumping its rain. Wind hurled through the trees and lightning streaks darted across the sky. Neither Princess nor I were very fond of such electric displays of nature. It was always a race to see who could jump into who's lap first at the initial clapping of thunder and streaks of lightning. Again, within seconds I felt her presence and I knew she had returned to accompany me through this first of storms since she had transcended this life. An absorbing calm filled the room as we weathered the storm together. I could really talk with Princess; she was right there with me. A few hours later when the storm subsided Princess was gone and I was, once again, left all alone.

There have been several returns since those early days. Sometimes I *will* her to return, but it is only in my mind that I have summoned her presence. These welcomed return visits, these special times of her reemergence, seem to come at no particular beckoning from within me. Lasting anywhere from several minutes to several hours, I savor those moments of togetherness and then she's on her

Mom, I'm okay, I can play
  I can run in the sun.
Please don't cry, I can fly
  It's really fun and you're the one
I am watching, keeping track...
  Now look forward, don't look back.
I'm your angel, now it's true
  Just remember, I'll always love you.
I'm by your side Mom, every day
  I go with you in work and in play.
I know you love me, you always will
  And my love for you grows greater still.
Our years together haven't ended, Mom...
  We'll always be together.

way.

Some might say it is all in my mind, but if those doubters ever had a first hand experience, they too would know of what I speak. Although Princess is physically gone I know that she lives, as sure as I know my own name. Because of this, the days have become more bearable, a little eaiser to accept and a lot brighter. The pain continues almost a year later, but it is being transformed from affliction to consolation.

There are times when the pain is razor sharp and cuts through the stillness of the night, causing tears to roll down my face in a quiet search for tranquility. At these times I try to focus on all that we shared, the beauty of our lives together and the loving bond that lives on...a bond that time cannot erase. I must remember that she is now healthy and happy and released from the deplorable affliction of her physical restriction. Also at this moment I must remember that God gives us His love, and something or someone to love He only lends us. Nine beautiful years, nine years of unconditional companionship. And that is what I concentrate on today.

I once read the story of the loaves and fishes, the feeding of the several thousand, from a different perspective. It concentrated on the resources possessed, the few loaves and fishes, rather than on the lack. As I recall this story, I realize that I must focus on all that we had and in a very real sense still have, rather than on what has been taken from us. What we shared then and what we share today time cannot erase. That will be with us forever.

Princess, I miss you
    But I know that you're near.
It's been nine long months now
    But I sense you are here.
Like many times before
    Without words when we'd talk
You still speak to me
    Every day as I walk.
Each night as I surrender
    To sleep as it comes.
I feel you here with me
    We still share our bond.
There's never a moment, Babe
    You're not in my heart.
Nothing, sweet Princess,
    Can keep us apart.

PART II

God is love...
And all love for any one of His creatures
    is from Him...
    and with Him
    and continues to live.

PREPARATION FOR THE END

Princess and I were given a very special gift, a grace period of eight months from September through April. It was a time that allowed us to speak freely of death and it enhanced our ability to experience life more fully in the time we had left. It was important for us to acknowledge the truth. Truth does set us free; by denying truth we are held in bondage. It was a relief to share rather than restrain our feelings and emotions; to cry together and give each other what we had to offer of strength and tenderness. Our convenant together was reaffirmed and allowed us to proceed with living.

Perhaps some people can survive the loss of their pet without feeling the enormous pain I felt, but for many more others I suspect it is a tragedy followed by deep sorrow and a multitude of emotional responses. These emotions respect no boundaries; they touch male and female, young and old, rich and poor, single and married and healthy and sick.

Each of us responds differently to grief, suffering and change, but we do respond. We never recover from the death of a loved one or a loved pet totally because they have been a part of our lives that will always remain in memory. Expecting it to be otherwise jeoparizes our own healing. You and your pet's journey of life together will always be

remembered, even when you are no longer together.

Time is an important part of the healing process
and there is really no way to speed up the process
or to bypass the piercing pain. But time alone
doesn't heal. The only way we can come to final
acceptance is to allow ourselves the time necessary
and to work through our emotions as they surface.
Time heals when we value our own life and believe
in our ability to find new life in the days ahead. The
suffering and pain we experience in our loss can
help us to grow if we are open to it. These
experiences can make us gentle, caring, loving,
compassionate people if we so choose to respond.

Losing your pet is a major transition time in your
life. It is a time of personal uprooting, but it can
also open the door to a new and richer life. New
beginnings are not simple or easy or comfortable.
They challenge us. I speak from my own experience
just as you can speak from yours. With faith, even
when walking in the shadow of darkness and the
valley of death, I knew somewhere deep inside I did
have the courage to choose life again, to go on
living. And through all the pain I found that
courage.

It is impossible to prepare for a crisis after it
occurs. If you are given the gift of time, as Princess
and I were, you can begin to prepare before death
calls. We had done some of the grieving together
and in a very real way the journey towards healing
had already begun. If your pet's death was
unexpected, there isn't time to prepare beforehand
and the grieving beings when the loss occurs. Either
way, there is much coping that lies ahead.
Although we each experience our loss in a uniquely

personal way, there are certain phases that we all go through when faced with any crisis and it helps to understand them. It is also important to realize that crisis brings out the best and worst in us. It is unreal to expect otherwise or to think there are no dark corners lurking in the background to cause miscommunication, misunderstanding and hurt feelings even in the most loving and supportive families.

In Part II we will look at some of the responses to crises. I hope they will help you in your own journey towards healing, and perhaps give you a better understanding of yourself and others who experience the loss of their pets.

DISATTACHMENT

Disattachment, or distancing yourself from your pet, is sometimes an emotional response; a way of trying to lessen the pain of the known outcome. It is often a normal response on the heels of denial. It may seem upon first thought to be one way of softening the blow of the inevitable death, but the more we remove ourselves from it, the less acceptable death is and it becomes more difficult to cope and move towards healing.

Disattachment can take many forms. It may begin with something as simple as ignoring your pet's greeting when you arrive home, or it may involve termination of those special "you and your pet" talks. If your pet is still able to actively run and play, it may mean that you no longer go out together for walks or romp on the floor in play. If allowed to go too far, it can eventually lead to all but ignoring your pet, except for the regular feedings and trips outdoors. Whatever form it takes, if allowed to continue, it will most certainly lead to guilt after your pet is gone. And because this disattachment puts stress on your pet, it could lead to further complications.

The protective distancing or silencing is a waste of the quality time that you have left together. I found myself at one point beginning to distance myself from Princess. Almost unconsciously I was putting up an invisible barrier thinking that if I began letting go now, it wouldn't be so hard later on. Fortunately I quickly realized what was happening and actually moved closer to Princess. I wanted to help her live, really live, until death. We worked together to treat her as a whole person, not just someone who was going to die. I knew I wanted us both to live our remaining time together rather than wait out death.

Another form of disattachment can be acquiring another pet before your ailing pet is gone. Not only can this sometimes cause disattachment for you, but it may be difficult on your long-time companion when he is least equipped to cope with the new-comer and your divided attention.

If you catch yourself in the initial stages of disattachment, reconsider your involvement. We each respond differently and we must go through the experience according to how we feel. Maybe for some people this disattachment is necessary, but if you realize you are distancing yourself and you feel this is not how you want to respond, then actively take steps to put yourself back into the relationship. Rather than move away, spend some quality time each day with your pet and talk through your feelings with your special animal friend. In retrospect, those times when Princess and I tuned out the world and tuned in to each other are some of the most special memories. Knowing that we lived fully to the end gives me much comfort today. I'm sure that had we not maintained our closeness the guilt would have been, and continue to be, very strong today.

Yes, it was difficult when I looked into Princess' eyes and saw her looking back lovingly not to think of the inevitable. Oh how I wished the disease would go away and that she could live on for many years...but denying it wouldn't help and distancing myself from her would only cause greater pain. Deep down I knew that. When a human is terminally ill many people find it difficult to face that person. They don't know what to say or to do and they withdraw, later feeling guilty for abandoning that person. I have never felt that I abandoned Princess or gave her any less attention, affection or love. Today that stands as a very real symbol and memory of our special covenant.

THE MOMENT OF REALITY: IMPACT

"Spinal myelopathy." Although the neurosurgeon spoke these words softly, aware that I knew the inevitable outcome of the diagnosis, they pounded like a jackhammer over and over in my head. Then seven months later, death.

The impact, that moment of knowing, whether it be a proclamation with many days to follow or the sudden impact of an accidental death, is often accompanied by shock. At this moment a sort of numbness envelops you which is nature's way of cushioning the impact. This numbness may cause physical responses such as loss of appetite or the feeling that your stomach is tied in knots. You may even feel that you are not really with it, a spaced-out sort of feeling. You may find yourself responding and acting out of habit. When it is the normal time for feeding you may catch yourself heading for the pet's food to prepare it, attempting to do the routine things you did together for years. You may go through the motions of your normal routine and hardly remember doing those things. You may walk around the yard where you once played together so often, repeating over and over to yourself, "What will I do? How can I make it? This is not wallowing in self-pity, nor is it selfish. You are simply being human. The days ahead of quiet desperation must be worked through. It is a difficult process and to expect to walk away from the death in good, strong, positive spirits, no matter how much faith you may have, is as ridiculous as expecting a patient to get up off the operating table and walk away after hours of major surgery.

You can expect to be in shock for awhile and sometimes the emotional numbness that accompanies this state is a little frightening. You may feel like you have lost control. You can't believe this is happening to you, but you must struggle to accept the reality. It is real. It has happened. And you will survive. The pain you are feeling is normal and it is proof you are alive. How sad it would be to go through the motions of living without the ability to feel. Know that because you have the ability to feel pain, you also have the ability to get to the other side and feel joy again. During this time allow yourself to feel the pain, to experience it. Move toward it rather than move away from it. It is not bottomless and you won't get lost in it, although right now you may feel that it will have no end. It is important for your healing that you allow yourself to experience all the feelings that accompany your loss. They are normal, natural and they are actually helpful. The numbness will soon wear off and the real grieving will begin.

During those first few hours, or before if there has been time to prepare, there are decisions to be made as to what you will do with the body. You have several choices and the one you choose depends upon your own preference. You can leave the decision to your veterinarian as to how to dispose of the body, or you can choose a burial site that is special and holds great meaning for you or your pet. Today there are pet cemetaries in most areas of the United States, allowing for a private cemetery burial, or a communal cemetery burial. Another option is cremation for your pet, as I chose to do, because I wanted to have Princess' ashes returned to me. Most places offering cremation provide either individual cremation or communal cremation, which is less expensive. Only you and your family can decide what is best for you.

DENIAL

After the initial shock, a common and very normal response is denial. You have intellectually comprehended the situation, what has actually happened, or you have been given the time-limiting news of impending death. Yet inside you deny what is happening. Denial functions much as a buffer against the loss, allowing us to collect ourselves, and with time, to activate other coping mechanisms.

Denial began for me before impact, when Dave told me there was a probability of spinal myelopathy even before the actual diagnosis was made. Although he was pretty sure it was not a disc problem (which meant something entirely different, a problem we could have dealt with that didn't mean death), I chose to believe it really was a disc. Princess couldn't possibly have this other dreaded, foreign condition. Yet always lingering in the back of my mind was the ominous possibility of hearing the neurosurgeon announce "spinal myelopathy." It was denial that kept me from scheduling an appointment with the neurosurgeon earlier. Somehow if I just didn't have to hear it, it would go away and Princess could go on living normally.

Another form of denial that sometimes comes into play after we become aware of impending death is bargaining. Bargaining is the term used when a person makes a statement of sacrifice if only the pet will be allowed to live, such as "If he lives, I'll never miss his regular walks again," or "If she lives, I'll never put her in a kennel or leave her alone," or "I'll promise to do this or that if my pet can live." Obviously these bargaining sacrifices are a last attempt at hope that our pet's life can continue on. Unfortunately, life doesn't begin or end on bargains and sooner or later we must come to terms with the reality of the situation. Nevertheless, this is a stage many people go through.

Even if you experience denial before death, as I did, denial may make another visit after death has occurred. I remember thinking so many times when I was conducting a training session or speaking engagement that I had to get home to feed Princess. Then the reality hit once again. No, I can't feed Princess, she's not at home.

The depth of denial for some will be dependent upon how much you need and want your beloved pet with you. You may even feel, as I did with Princess, that you can't go on or don't want to go on without your pet. I couldn't imagine life without her and many times after she was gone I actually felt it would be easier to die myself and go be with her than to go on living on this earth.

It takes time to work through denial and there is no specific timetable for getting over it, but as you work through it remember that it is important for you to do what feels right for you as you gradually progress toward acceptance. In time you will find that you can face the reality. There will probably always be a part of you that grieves, but you will be able to accept the death and begin to live again.

I have kept Princess' pictures around me, as well as her ashes. To me this is not a denial of the reality; rather it is a healthy affirmation of the love we shared and that continues today. I can't deny my loss and the void that remains, but I can choose not to dwell on it. Denial is dangerous if allowed to continue, especially if it is an attempt to stifle the grieving process. Grieving will take place in any event, but if denied or suppressed, the healing power grieving can bring will not be effectively activated. Denial allows us to test the reality of a new situation, absorbing only those aspects that we are ready to accept without being totally devastated. Reality will eventually make its way through to you as you accept the fact that your pet is gone, and it will lead to healing.

We have been good at insulating ourselves from pain and death in our culture. There is a perceived, if not real, taboo in our society against speaking of death. Perhaps it occurs more with humans, but it happens with animals too. While I was going through the initial stages of numbness and grieving over the loss of Princess, I was very fortunate because most of the people around me were very supportive and understanding. They didn't sidestep the issue but were open and receptive, and allowed me to share whatever I was needing to share.

Some people, however, don't receive this support. It is as if others are denying your loss. Friends, relatives and acquaintances may try to change the subject as soon as it is approached, rather than confront and deal with it. Family members may find it quite difficult to speak to each other about the loss. This may be in part because the other persons are grieving differently than you or maybe they find it difficult to face their own emotions. We all have our own way of grieving and we don't necessarily parallel the grieving of another person, even within our own family. Outsiders who have never shared the special bond with a pet as you have may appear to be cold, uncaring or distant when in reality they simply cannot understand your grief. I had one such person, my boyfriend at the time, that simply could not understand. One afternoon, two weeks after Princess' euthanasia, I began crying because I was thinking of Princess and hurting. His response was, "What are you crying for?" When I told him, he then responded, "When are you ever going to get over this? It has been two weeks now." Obviously this person didn't understand. That was difficult for me to accept, and he was unwilling to allow me the space I needed and the time so necessary for grieving. If you have someone like this who doesn't understand your grief over the loss, find someone who does. It is important that you be able to talk about it, to express your feelings to someone who will listen. Psychologists and other counselors now know that we need as much support in the loss of a companion animal as in the loss of a human.

If you find it difficult to gain this support from

those around you, there are organizations and support groups today that are available to help you through the grieving process. These groups are generally comprised of people who have experienced the loss of their pet and who meet periodically to help each other through the many stages leading to healing. Expressing feelings to others who understand and have had similar experiences brings remarkable relief and helps you on the road to recovery. If you are not aware of any support groups in your area, a call to your veterinarian or humane society will probably give you that information. If you cannot locate a support group, private counseling is available from qualified counselors and psychologists.

Although I experienced denial before Princess' death, the importance of facing the truth together became very evident to me and I believed Princess knew that she would not live much longer. We couldn't deny the truth much longer and to do so would have been to waste the valuable time we had left together. Many times we talked and cried for hours as we sat cuddled together, my arms wrapped around her. Princess snuggled close and licked the tears as they trickled down my face as if to say, "We'll make it through this together, it will be okay." Being able to talk with her, sensing her knowing and understanding, lifted an enormous weight from me. Not all the weight, but much of it. It was a relief to share with her, not sidestepping or denying the reality. Because of our openness we were able to give each other all we had of strength and tenderness, love and care. It was as if by acknowledging the reality we could begin to come to terms with it together while she was still alive, and because of this I have never had a lingering feeling of leaving things left unsaid. The truth did set us free.

It might seem to others that I was overly preoccupied with the preparation for Princess' euthanasia, but it was a way of still exercising some control, of coming to grips with reality and beginning to work through the grieving process. I am grateful today for all the steps and time we took because it made the transition a little easier for me to go on afterwards without her physical presence.

Phone calls to family and friends increased during the early stages of my grieving because I needed to talk to others about what was happening...both before the euthanasia and after. I talked a lot to Princess too. Masking the truth through denial meant masking my love for Princess and rather than hide it, I wanted it to shine forth in all its beauty. I have always found it difficult to keep things in and have shared my feelings quite openly. No matter how painful those feelings are, talking through them is a way of lessening the burden they impose and diffusing the weight.

Our American tradition has valued independence and self-reliance. We are taught to manage ourselves and people often feel ashamed to admit to others their neediness or dependence. Perhaps it is difficult to accept or admit our neediness or help because it seems impossible to repay what is given to us in the form of loving support. Perhaps it is simply because we have forgotten that we do not exist independently in this world. We do need others, particularly in times of crisis and we don't have to go through everything alone. We are interdependent beings and we are diminished to the extent we deny this. We forget that saying yes to a gift of help and friendship is also giving a gift in return. A very special gift.

DEPRESSION

When the numbness wears off and the anger is exhausted, depression may be the next visitor. It, too, is a very natural response to grief or loss and in a sense it is the preparatory grief that we go through in order to prepare ourselves for accepting the loss. For weeks after Princess' euthanasia I felt empty and hollow, lethargic and depressed. Decisions were difficult and apathy and discouragement prevailed. I went about my business because I had to fulfill my obligations, but the feeling returned at the end of each assignment, at the end of each day, and continued its unwelcomed stay. I kept asking myself the question, "Will I ever feel better?" I felt like there were no walls left to lean on, no water in the well. It felt like I was at the end of the line.

I knew it was healthy to allow myself to express my feelings and I also knew that talking to someone who really cared and listened would help. I can't say it took away the pain, but I felt better when I was allowed to ramble and repeatedly talk through my feelings recalling what Princess and I shared. I needed people who would let me talk about my loss, who would listen without judging or saying, "It was only a dog, Cheryl, and you can get another one." There were a few people who couldn't understand how I felt because to them Princess was just a dog. Evidently they had never shared the incredible bond with a pet that Princess and I enjoyed. It was easy to resent these people, but I worked hard to fight that feeling and accept them for where they were. I had my family and many friends who really did understand my pain and they helped me just by being there. They were the ones who didn't try to ignore what had happened or pretend it didn't happen or say, "It's all over, now get on with your life."

It has been almost a year since Princess died and the down times return again and again, but not as often now and they don't last as long as they first did. Healing is a process and it sometimes takes months and even years, but it does come and the depression does pass. And it will come for you, too. I still have nights when I cry myself to sleep, but they are much less frequent now. When I see a German Shepherd on television, or when I'm out in the neighborhood and pass one on the street, the pain quickly returns. That's normal. I recall one day about six months after Princess' euthanasia when everywhere I went there were German Shepherds. I was on my way to visit a colleague, and crossing the street ahead of me was a man and a German Shepherd. A few hours later, driving between appointments, a truck ahead of me had two German Shepherds in the back. And yet a while later I stopped at a shopping mall and there was another German Shepherd in the car next to where I parked. I couldn't seem to get away from them. Needless to say, the pain again surfaced and the emptiness and void recurred all too vividly.

The intense pain and depression was vicious, but they were something I felt was necessary and that I had to feel to really express how much I loved Princess and give tribute to how very important she was to me. Somehow it seemed that if I didn't feel this, it would be a statement that I didn't really care and I would be letting go of the one last thing I had left of Princess. At times it was almost more than I could cope with and no amount of fighting it would bring relief. Remembering the children's nighttime prayer I grew up with, I might have well repeated it this way during those moments of incredible pain and depression:

Now I lay me down to sleep
I pray the Lord my soul to keep.
If I should die before I wake
I pray the Lord my soul to take...

...and maybe that would be easier
than facing a new day without Princess.

I did, however, discover for myself in the days ahead what I had been telling people all along in my training sessions on attitude and personal growth. When you are laughing and smiling, you can't be hurting at the same time. You can't hold a negative and a positive thought at the same time. Strange, but it is true. At first, I felt guilt again, how could I be laughing? How could I possibly be happy? But I found that I could, that it really was all up to me, my attitude and a little time. The key was understanding that being happy once again did not diminish or take away anything from what Princess and I shared.

Finally, almost a year later now, I no longer have the terrible bouts with depression. I do feel the pain emerge at times when I am caught off guard and I still miss Princess very, very much. But I am healing and I am once again living and looking forward with anticipation to each new day. I can finally be around other animals today, even German Shepherds, and really enjoy them and be happy with them. In fact, just a few weeks ago, I attended a dog show and had a wonderful time playing with all the dogs, especially the German Shepherds.

Depression does end; you will get better. Just give yourself a little time and don't hold on to the depression for the sake of being a martyr.

GRIEVING

Certainly we must and we do move forward with our life after the death of our beloved pet. But grieving is a necessary part of healing. It is a normal, appropriate response to loss and the healthy thing to do is to feel miserable for awhile. When you lose your pet, a part of your life has been severed by that loss and darkness, a symbol of loneliness and of being lost, prevails. Desperately we want and need to know that the long, grinding work of grieving will somehow, at sometime, end; and to know that you will smile and laugh again because you want to smile and laugh, not just because it is forced or expected by others.

Grieving can take many forms as we have already seen, but for most of us it also confuses, exhausts and seems at times to block our minds from the ability to think. The hours seem endless and blurred at first and the pain seems the heaviest. The hole in our heart is big enough to walk through. How can I face the days ahead? How can I live in this emptiness when I no longer feel like myself? The questions we ask ourselves are mindless, like trying to answer, "How many miles are there in a night?" or "Is life triangular or square?" Many of the questions that haunt us in our grief are like these; they just don't seem to have any answers or make any sense. Measured by clocks, calendars and watches, time is just one empty moment followed by another. And as you fall asleep, tears cover your pillow and you wake up the next morning to the dark reality of your new partners, mourning and grief.

Along with the obvious feelings of depression, sadness and pain, there are other reactions to our loss that may not be so obvious, such as feeling helpless, empty, pessimistic, irritable, angry, guilty and restless. We may find ourselves with the inability to concentrate, losing hope, motivation, energy and our sleep patterns are interrupted. Any or all of these are expected when you experience a loss.

Grieving is the period of mourning during which we come to terms with our loss and it is not all negative. It can, in fact, be very positive. Positive grieving is the experience of remembering the good, happy, fun-filled, loving memories. It is being glad for the life you had together and yes, wishing you still had that life. It is feeling sorrowful because your pet is no longer with you, but it is knowing there is still much happiness and joy to experience and life to be lived. Positive grieving is a right you have to feel and express your loss deeply and painfully. It says you are hurting because there is a hole in your life and it says that it is okay to cry, acknowledging the positive side of tears that give tribute to the life and love you shared.

Some people find it difficult to cry while others find it very easy and automatic. Whatever your situation, however, tears are usually a necessary release with a language all their own, appearing when we are overwhelmed with feelings that words cannot describe. Tears are actually helpful, a very real part of the cleansing and healing process. Repressed tears or repressed grief can lead to psychological disturbances and even physical illness. Sometimes people fight the tears vehemently because they are still in the denial stage; others simply believe that freedom to cry is not granted to adults. But not to cry when the tears are ready to be released means not coming to grips with your loss. It is like barring the doors of your heart, being unattached emotionally, like living in prison. Sometimes there is no other comfort, only tears and the deep pain...and the passage of time.

I found it necessary to allow myself a grieving time each day for several months. I needed this time before I could really let go and move on to greater healing. Usually my time was in the evening at the end of the day when no one else was around; when I could just be me and feel all I wanted to feel and yes, even to talk out loud to Princess. It was a time of remembering, a time of reliving those beautiful memories...but it was also a time of many questions that still went unanswered.

The period of grieving can take many months, but there will come a time when you are ready once again to say yes to life, to close the door softly but firmly on the past and move on...to know there is promise in the pain you are feeling. There is spring after winter, sun after rain. When we can recognize, accept and live through the myriad of emotions which accompany the grieving process it becomes an important phase of personal growth.

The grieving process provides the time needed to ventilate all our feelings and its purpose is to heal our mental and emotional wounds so we can be freed from the pain and begin the process of living positive, constructive lives in the present. The most significant sign that you are coming out of the grieving period is the feeling deep inside that says, "I have survived." Although there will be surges of nostalgia, tears that break through periodically and a return of the sinking feeling at times, the past no longer will dominate the present for you. In a way the sadness never ends. It strikes at unexpected moments, triggered by a picture, a special place revisited, a habit, a thought. But the time of intense, painful introspection can end if you want it to and when you are ready. Just as we prepare for winter each year, we also prepare for the spring, the time of new life and rebirth. You will move beyond grieving to new hope and new life.

There are many firsts that we travel through as we grieve. In fact, the first year is the hardest as we experience special days...Christmas, birthday, Thanksgiving, Fourth of July, Memorial Day...for the first time without our beloved pet. There are many times during the first year when we are caught off-guard, such as when we find a toy under a piece of furniture or hear someone talk about their pet. Periodically I find Princess' hair on a piece of clothing, or under a sofa cushion or some other hard to get at place, and it still stings. But it is also very special.

Now, as I think I am much better and healing, I am rapidly approaching the anniversary of Princess' departure from this world. How appropriate it is that this first anniversary falls on Good Friday. There is an anniversary reaction triggered by the date itself, but I know that while it will bring pain once again, I can choose to experience it as a special time of remembrance to carry me through the dark and back into the light.

You will continue to miss your beloved pet, as I do Princess...that will go on. But the dark night, the anguish of grief and the agony will end. Maybe now it doesn't seem possible to ever be whole again, but you will be, someday. There are still those unguarded moments when I'm torn apart anew, maybe there always will be. But I know that if it weren't for the wonderful life shared there would not be those moments...and in that way they too have become very special. Once we have moved through the greatest part of the grieving process these periodic times of sadness and pain are no longer all encompassing and do not pull us back into the past and away from the present.

When your pet dies it is almost like a part of you goes with them. But you will go on living and move towards healing. It takes time, but it will happen. Give yourself that time...you deserve it. An emotional wound requires the same attention as a physical wound. As you proceed in your journey of healing, when the loneliness and emptiness surround you...stop. Stop exactly where you are and give yourself a chance to be aware of something good, something beautiful. Maybe it is the sound of a bird singing, a daffodil peeking up through the ground, the magnificence of a sunset, children laughing...or just the quiet realization of the miracle of life. Give yourself room to experience the smallest awareness, the tiniest symbol of hope and new life. Often at these times I find myself remembering the lesson Princess taught me...to stop and examine, to stop and be aware, to stop for just a moment and drink in the wonder of life itself...of new growth, of birth, of song...of living. These moments are very special and remind me that Princess still lives as part of me. That will always be. And that is progress.

CHILDREN AND PET LOSS

Facing death, the loss of a pet, is no easier for children than adults. In fact, sometimes a child's ability to face the loss is complicated by parents or other adults who are finding it difficult to cope themselves. When this occurs, children may become more confused and not know how they are to express their feelings or which ones are okay to express. Few people feel comfortable talking about death, and having to deal with it directly and talk with a child about it may make it even more uncomfortable. Obviously, the child's age and level of understanding will make a difference in the communication process and ability to comprehend the death. For example, a child of three, four or five may not feel the death is permanent. Like a bulb planted that brings forth new life in the Spring, a small child may believe that his pet will come home again.

If the death comes slowly, as with Princess, time is available to begin talking about the impending death while the pet is still somewhat healthy. The more grief can be expressed before death, the less unbearable it will be afterwards. If the child is protected by artificial barriers or untruths, it will stifle any preparatory grief which opens the door to the healing process. Although the loss, regardless of preparation, will be traumatic, the trauma can be magnified if the child is not allowed to talk and cry together with his parents or other significant adults in his life. When you can share together in this preparatory process you will gradually face the reality and come to an acceptance together.

As you discuss the impending loss with your child, remember that each person reacts different- ly...from silent withdrawal and isolation to a loud mourning which desires replacement. Each child's grieving is different and may take one or many forms of expression. A normally playful and active child may become withdrawn and sullen, moods may change quickly and you may not know what triggered the emotional swing. A child may ex- perience physical responses such as stomachaches and other complaints, often signaling the need for more attention. He may invent stories of how his pet is still alive, make up things they have done together, or play as though the pet is still alive but now invisible. Tears may be triggered by something that is said, by a television program or simply by thinking about his pet. He may ask questions like "Why don't dogs or cats live as long as people?" And when you think you have heard it all and acceptance has been achieved, you're asked another question that seems to come from nowhere and is totally unrelated to what is happening or being discussed at the time.

Just as adults sometimes feel guilt, children may also feel guilt. They may even feel responsible for their pet's death, no matter how irrational that feeling may be. At these times, it is important to remember that feelings are neither right nor wrong; they just are. Helping the child begin to work through the process and come to an understanding that it was not his fault is important. If reprimanded or corrected harshly, the child may hold the grief inside which can be the roots of later emotional disturbance.

As you discuss the inevitable outcome, telling the child not to be sad is in a sense asking him not to think about the impending death. We are all sad when we lose someone we love, and the child is in the process of losing what he loves. If allowed to experience and express his sorrow, acceptance of the reality will be easier, but don't force the child to talk about it. If he resists any discussion, leave the door open. Denial, just as with adults, is normal for children and they shouldn't be judged for this response. The denial may be evidenced by disattachment, too. Letting him know that you are willing to talk and letting him see you express your sorrow will help pave the way for him to be able to express and deal with his emotions. Seeing you express your own feelings may give him the signal he needs to validate his own feelings of pain. He needs to know it is okay to cry and to have deep feelings. When he is ready to open up and share his feelings, he will as long as he thinks it is safe to do so. Sometimes when a child has not been able to express his feelings, it is helpful if you let him know that you understand his pain and grief. Often you can help reassure him and pave the way for him to open up to you simply by being present with the touch of a hand, a stroke across the hair or just sitting in silence with the child. Perhaps a few simple words would help, such as, "I know you must be hurting—want to talk?" or "I'd like to listen if you want to talk." It requires an understanding of the child's needs and being attuned to his feelings to help him diminish guilt and any fear of retribution.

At the time of death it is important to take your cues from your child. If it is possible, and they feel the need, it may be helpful to allow the child to stroke the head and body and feel the stillness of his deceased pet. This shouldn't be forced, but if the child wants to touch and see his pet, it may help him to understand the reality, and move away from denial into acceptance.

After the death, especially when there is little or no time to prepare, children may be angry and we need to allow them expression of those feelings. They, too, go through the stages of bitterness, numbness, anger and all the rest just like adults. If the child becomes angry, tolerate anger within reason and help him take the steps towards acceptance without guilt. The void and emptiness after the loss is deep and children need someone to talk with as much as before. Remember that the loss of a pet fish, or turtle or guinea pig is just as great to the child as the loss of a dog or cat to an adult. We need to help them over the initial shock and guilt feelings to prepare for gradual accep-tance. Don't force the reality, though. This was an unexpected and unacceptable event and it will take time.

The attempt to come to terms with death is a lifelong process for most people. I don't believe anyone understands death fully, no matter how much faith or anything else we have. We know that we go on, but just how that is accomplished and what it will be like is something no one can answer. Because this is true we need to leave room for doubt, questions and differences of opinion. Here it is important, I feel, to be sure we give truthful answers as best we can so they can be built on later as the child comes to understand death more fully, rather than quick answers to satisfy the moment which must be unlearned and discarded later because they were false.

No matter how much you discuss the loss with your child, the child will no doubt hear what he is willing to hear and accept only that which he is ready to accept at the time. And that is okay. The thoughts you share are seeds that will grow with time. If you keep the channels of communication open, your child will be able to share the questions, fears, confusion and anxiety as they surface. Whatever you tell your child, they will know if you are being sincere, and they will find out the truth in a painful way later if not told the truth initially. It is better not to deceive than to have the child grow roots of anger because of the deception when he was younger.

At the time of death, the truth in its simplest form is probably safest. Your child's response will tell you whether or not he needs to know more right then. If you are not sure what they want to know, ask a question in return before you answer. And if you don't have an answer, admit it. More than ever before your child will need to be able to trust the people with whom he shares his feelings and curious questions. As he gets older, you may find he asks questions that return to the loss, even years later. Children don't easily forget and as they are ready to hear more, those questions will surface.

I am reminded of a friend who once told me of a situation where a young child was told he would be put to sleep to have a tonsillectomy. Later, when his dog was sick and had to be euthanized, he was told that his dog had to be put to sleep. Obviously, statements like these can cause much confusion for the child as to the meaning of euthanasia and not returning.

Providing another pet for a child is often helpful. Having another pet on which to focus his attention may help in easing some of the pain, as well as allowing him to begin rebuilding the closeness and companionship he enjoyed with his deceased friend. Where adults sometimes feel they just don't want another pet because it couldn't replace the one that has died, or because they don't want to go through the pain of another loss, a child often reacts very positively and welcomes the new pet with renewed enthusiasm. Even if it is met with early resistance, usually the barriers quickly diffuse and they are eager once again to share their love and affection.

GUILT

When we experience the loss of our pet we sometimes experience feelings of guilt stemming from many factors. Added to the already intense pain, guilt is a very heavy burden and makes the process of grieving and healing much more difficult and hinders the ability to achieve closure.

Many times a person experiences a great amount of anger, and when that anger turns inward it often becomes guilt. Anger often is expressed by verbal statements directed at the veterinarian such as "You told me you were going to take care of her; now she's dead," or "You don't even care, she's just another dog to you." These angry kinds of statements, made because of hurt and pain, often result in guilt later. If you feel your veterinarian is cold or distant, remember that the death of your pet is also stressful to him or her, and disattachment, as discussed earlier, may also be one way of coping for your veterinarian.

A sudden or accidental death, as well as a prolonged illness or disease before death, can foster guilt feelings of *"if only."* I had these feelings for a long time. *If only* I had done something differently, maybe Princess wouldn't have developed spinal myelopathy. *Maybe if* I'd taken her to the neuro-

94

surgeon earlier, we could have changed it. If onlys and maybes played through my mind feeding on themselves and creating more if onlys. Although the doctors told me there was no known cause and it couldn't be changed or reversed, even with earlier diagnosis, I still felt guilty. Somehow I couldn't help but feel that I had not done enough and that I had let Princess down. Princess had always been given an incredible amount of attention and love. I always fed her well and gave her plenty of vitamins. She received daily exercise and had all her routine vaccinations and check-ups on schedule. I knew intellectually that I had taken the best care of her that I knew how to give, yet I still felt guilty.

You may feel this tremendous burden of guilt because you were not watching when your pet was outside playing close to the street, or because you left the door open accidentally which resulted in your pet being hit by a car. Maybe it stems from feelings that you didn't spend enough time with your pet or because you never got around to doing the things together that you were always going to do someday. Guilt can also rear its ugly head when you recall the harsh words you uttered in moments of frustration or anger. Children, too, experience guilt and sometimes we can sentence them to years of guilt by not telling the truth about their pet's death. I know of one person whose parents did not tell him his dog had been struck by a car and killed. Instead they told him that he had left the door open and his dog got out and wandered off. Not until he was twenty-eight did he finally discover the truth. As a result, he carried intense feelings of guilt all those years because he thought he had been the cause of losing his pet.

Guilt is also a very real part of our emotions when we must be the one to make the decision for euthanasia. I really struggled with this. I kept asking myself, "Why do I have to make this decision? It's not mine to make. I can't be the one to say it is time to die. Was it really my decision to make?" I wanted so much to do what was right for Princess, but the decision was so difficult. I knew it was cruel to let her go on living in her condition, but still it was a very, very difficult decision to make.

From the moment I called Dave on Monday to schedule the euthanasia until the actual day, Thursday, I lived every moment with guilt and the questions heavy on my heart. As I shared in the first part of this book, I was given a sign on Thursday morning that clearly indicated this was the right decision. Sometimes, however, even today I forget about this sign and the guilt suddenly returns. It is then I must stop and rationally remember all the reasons why it was the best decision I could have made under the circumstances. I think the most difficult part was that I wanted her to be able to make the decision, I didn't want to have this kind of control over life and death. Next to actually losing Princess and having to make the decision, this feeling of guilt was the hardest thing I had to cope with and resolve within myself. In the end, what we really need to know is that it wasn't our fault. We keep asking ourselves, did I do everything I could?

Let's look at the other side of guilt, the kind of guilt that results when what you did or didn't do resulted in the death of your pet or contributed to the death. Perhaps your pet darted in front of your car or was sitting under the car when you drove off. Or maybe you didn't follow the doctor's instructions and your pet's health worsened, or he didn't pull through a delayed surgery that could have been done much earlier and maybe even saved the life of your pet. Whatever the reason, the devastation guilt can cause comes when you pronounce yourself with a verdict of guilty and continue the self-punishment. This can only lead to greater self-destruction and increased pain.

If you are feeling guilty and you also believe there is a legitimate reason for that guilt, it is important to work through and resolve it. Actually, there are four responses we can have. Three are unhealthy and lead to greater guilt and self-degradation. The fourth is a healthy, healing response.

First, you can deny it. Sometimes this involves suppressing the guilt feelings and in other situations it may include projecting the blame onto others. This, however, only drives it deeper into the subconscious mind where it can creep out when you least expect it and in destructive forms you may not even recognize or acquaint with the actual loss of your pet. Second, you can try to rationalize or justify the action that produced the guilt, but this doesn't work for very long because it won't convince your emotions and your feelings. The third way of responding to guilt is by focusing and dwelling upon it, but this usually results in the individual sinking deeper and deeper into depression.

The fourth way is the healthy response to guilt and the only way reconciliation occurs. This is to recognize and accept that you are guilty, then forgive yourself. Realize that what happened, happened and no amount of worry or guilt will change it. Open yourself to your humanity and imperfection. Forgive yourself for your imperfection and respect yourself enough to accept that forgiveness. Time takes care of many things, but it doesn't diminish unresolved guilt. And unresolved guilt continues its damage year after year.

Accept yourself and understand that imperfections and mistakes are a part of life, of being human. When guilt is recognized and faced for what it is, it opens us to God's unconditional love, to reconciliation and to healing. And when we are opened to this, it can become growth producing.

CLOSURE

Letting go is a struggle most of us face with the loss of our pets. It forces us to change, to let go of what was and the many things that were a part of our relationship, and accept new things of today. As long as we remain emotionally bound by the past, we cannot live in the present.

One way of letting go involves closure, that is, putting the past behind where it will stay; where it has its place. If we slam the door in anger on the past, it will bounce back open. If we nudge it indecisively, it won't close. We must, therefore, close it firmly and gently. In order to do this we must accept the past for what it was or has been. No one can can take away from us what we shared with our pets. But no amount of wishing we hadn't experienced the loss will change it. We must accept it. Sometimes it is difficult to let go because we don't want to lose what we had with our pet...the unconditional love, the companionship, the fun things we did together. Closure does not mean denying or diminishing the past. It just means we are not living there any more.

Regardless of the nature of death, it is important to acknowledge the loss, to give some closure, to say yes to the reality and yes to the life that is ahead for you. The people who help the most through this process are the ones who are willing to listen to your feelings. They are the ones who don't need to change the subject at the first sign of tears, and those who can share their own feelings of loss and pain. They are those who risk coming and being with you, even when they don't know what to say...knowing that just being there helps.

A burial or ceremonial service can be an important ritual to acknowledge the life, the loss, the love shared and the grief for adults as well as children. Each person needs to say goodbye in their own way and we must be sensitive to this. Unless some ritual is part of the ending, closure may be difficult to achieve. Burial rites can be very helpful to encourage the mourning process so necessary to be able to move on with life. It helps bring closure and the beginning of healing as it symbolizes outwardly what is taking place inside.

An important part of beginning the closure for me was actually being with Princess during the euthanasia. It helped me feel that I had done all I could and that I was with her to the end. Those who have the strength to sit with their pet in silence that goes beyond words during the euthanasia and for the moments afterwards may find, as I did, that the moment of death is neither frightening for themselves or painful for the pet...rather it is a peaceful transition. This isn't right for everyone, but I know for me it was necessary and it also helped bring closure. Having shared this with Princess I am quite certain that if given the same opportunity next time, I'll again be there to the end.

If you find closure difficult, try writing a closing letter to your pet. Include anything and everything you want to say. Some things you might address are how much you miss your pet, how much you love him and how much he meant to you. Talk about the privilege of sharing your life together. If there are any apologies needed, express them. Perhaps there are other feelings such as relief that their pain is over, hurt or loneliness or even bitterness or anger. Whatever your feelings, write them in a letter of closure. Finally, bid your pet farewell, except for the memories and the love that continues...the past is over.

Journal writing was another aid in my letting go and bringing closure. I didn't write daily, but I wrote whenever I felt the need. It was a very cathartic process for me allowing reflection and honesty in dealing with and facing my feelings. In a way it was an expression of my courage and desire to grow and move to new horizons. It has been an unending adventure into the mystery of my own unrepeatable relationship with Princess, as well as with myself; an adventure that continues today. This journal writing has become a record of my inward journey. Setting aside the time to write in my journal allowed me to perceive new depths and to discover unexpected connections and fresh insights about myself, my feelings and my relationship with Princess. It could be described as many things: A voyage, a mountain climb, an opening of new doors, a becoming, a probing and in a very real sense an answering to the call of my spirit. Most of all, it has been very healing.

Remaining distraught for a long period of time isn't proof that you really loved. Don't feel bound to hold the pain any longer than it is really there and remember that real love gives life, celebrates life. It doesn't ask for constant pain, rather it moves us on to renewed joy and happiness, and being joyful once again does not mean disloyalty or betrayal. Life would be dull and lifeless without hope and optimism, but it must be coupled with reality. Reality means looking at a situation as it is, not as you would like it to be and evaluating the situation honestly based on past and present experience.

It is hard to close the door, but it is necessary for your own well-being and for your continued growth. It has been difficult for me, as it might be for you. But in order to go on living and be able to allow the loving memories to continue, it was necessary for me to put them into proper perspective. When I was finally able to do this, I realized that what Princess and I had together lives on even stronger today and stands as a reason to move forward. When Princess died, she was the one who died and she didn't ask me to die with her. In fact, knowing her as I do, if she were able to put into words what her feelings are, I'm sure she would say, "Mom, just know always that I love you and that love will live on. Go on now, and remember what we shared. Let the joy, the love and the lessons of life we learned together give you the will to move forward and enjoy each day of life as it is given to you. Say yes to life, celebrate it and it will be a most beautiful tribute to me to have been part of helping you to a greater awareness of the richness life holds and understanding of what life really is."

Closure is allowing the loss to take an exit from your present and a cherished place in your past... and in your memory. It is not denial. Again, closure does not mean forgetting or even trying to forget what you shared, nor is it a denial of your loving devotion. Rather, closure is healthy and allows you to move forward and live in the present while always holding those memories close to your heart. You spent many years together. Those years were a very real part of your life and that will always be.

Remember not the events of the past,
the things of long ago consider not;
See, I am doing something new?
Now it springs forth, do you not perceive it?
In the desert I make a way,
in the wasteland, rivers.

Isaiah 43: 18, 19
New American Bible

GROWTH

In every situation of adversity, growth, strength and renewal of life occur as we confront the darkness of the experience, not when we avoid it. There is an old myth that time heals all wounds. But time, by itself, will not heal the pain and the grief unless you work through it. When you do, the grief can be transformed into personal growth. You can actually become something more than you were.

Although you must accept your pet's death, you don't need to sever all ties. You can build on the memories and allow those memories, the one thing no one can ever take from you, to enrich your life. They have become a part of you and will live on forever.

Never a day goes by that I don't think of Princess and recall moments we shared. Her memory lives on and because it does I can face the new day with renewed spirit and enthusiasm. Princess' life was a beautiful song, and if I want the spirit of what she stood for to live on, then I must remember this: *If her song is to continue, then I must do the singing.* Princess was so giving, so filled with life, and I'm sure she would encourage me to go on living, being happy and fulfilled.

I'm reminded of a wall hanging (still hanging in

my home today) that I made when Princess was just a puppy…

The world is such that
what appears to be an end
is really a new beginning.

Because of this, we can confidently say that our pain and suffering is never in vain. Much can be gained from our pain and suffering. We can be better prepared to comfort others. We can learn that we can put our trust in someone greater than ourselves. We can learn to give thanks in all things. It wasn't an accident that Princess came into my life. She was part of a greater plan and purpose, one that included suffering and pain and endings. But there can be no beginnings without endings. As hard as that is to accept sometimes, it is true. Life is a process of giving up and letting go and to not accept those changes when they come is to stifle growth and cause even deeper pain. To hang on to what isn't is to negate life; to live in the present and accept what is today is to grow and celebrate life.

I have come to look at the pain I endured not as a negative, not as something to try to rid myself of totally. Rather, I realize it is woven into the fabric of my life as one of the threads I must live and grow through. This has been one ending without which there could be no beginnings.

I never wanted this to happen, but I can't change it. What I can change is my attitude and response towards it. I can hold to the beautiful memories and shared experiences. The love we shared has a personal significance that has not only touched me deeply, but it has changed me. I have grown in many ways and as I continue to grow I uncover even more of the treasures Princess left with me. So many examples of a life lived fully emerge from day to day and I am reminded to take hold of that, to live it out...to really live in the present just as Princess did.

The first few months after Princess' death I had a hard time thinking about getting another dog. Somehow it seemed that I would be trying to replace her and I knew that was impossible. No other animal could take her place. I've grown through this now and just as a parent can have a second child and not love the first any less, so too can I go on to love another pet, without diminishing my love for Princess. This was hard for me to accept and it has taken time to work through.

Growth isn't always easy, and it isn't always pleasant. But it is the only way to live life fully. Just as life is a process, so too is growth. In life we meet obstacles, roadblocks, setbacks and reverses along the way. The loss of our loved pets are very real setbacks. But just as we cope and find solutions to our problems in life, rising to meet the challenge, so too will we learn to cope with our loss. I remember a saying that I have heard for years...it is simply this: *God gives us love, something to love He lends us.*

Be thankful for the time you had to spend on this earth with your pet. Cherish that time and hold those memories closely in your heart, but be willing to grow through your pain and suffering. Healing is there waiting if you will accept it, and you will emerge a stronger, more caring, more loving person because of your pain...*because of your love.*

FAITH

I couldn't complete this book without acknowledging the role of faith, for it was my faith that has been the constant throughout this time of anticipation, loss, grieving and gradual healing.

Why Princess? Why now? These were my words. These may also be the words you cried in painful desperation, or words you have yet to utter. Questions. Bottomless questions seeking answers, but there aren't any answers. These are the questions that hit hardest and linger the longest, whether death comes after a slow process as Princess' disease was, or an unexpected or accidental sudden death. I don't know that there are any answers. I'm no closer to the answers today than I was when I first asked the questions. But I feel I've grown in understanding and acceptance in so many other ways through the bitter pain and sorrow because of my faith. And I've also come to understand and accept that it is okay not to have all the answers.

As a Christian, I've tried to live my life in a way that gives testimony to my faith and witness to this commitment. I've believed that God cares for each of us and for each one of our pets...indeed for all His creatures great and small. (Matthew 10:29 tells us He sees every little sparrow fall.) I've believed in the power of prayer, and I have prayed not just at the end of the day, but throughout the day as I make this journey of life. I've taken quiet time for myself each day to hear what God is saying to me personally through silent listening and scripture. I've tried to live the commandment of love. Yet not one of these changed the ultimate result...my loss of Princess. So where am I today? I still believe in all this, and more.

One thing has become very clear to me over the past several months and it is simply this. Until we come to terms with death ourselves, it will be more difficult to come to terms with the death of a pet or a human loved one. Obviously most little children have no real concept of death and are unable to understand it at their early ages, so I am speaking here of adults. Each of us must come to terms with death. I can't give you my beliefs to hold as your own; you must find your own way. What is right for me may not be right for you, but I do want to share how my faith has affected my ability to cope with the loss of Princess, and how the loss of Princess has affected my faith. I'm sure there are many people who may disagree with some of my personal beliefs, but I can only say that they have come as a result of great searching, deep meditation, much prayer and personal experience.

I have believed in life after death for humans for many, many years. We are told in the Bible that there is salvation. It is not my purpose here to determine who salvation is for, or on what terms it is given. That has been argued for many years by many people. But I had questions about animals and other creatures of God. Deep in my heart I just felt...no, I believed...that God would not allow life, in any form, to die forever. That just doesn't fit my image of a sensitive and loving God. In fact, death in Aramaic means *not here, present somewhere else.*

Nevertheless, if you've ever been with a person at the moment of death, perhaps you've asked the same questions I have pondered many times. Where does the person go? I mean, the body is there, you can see that. But that isn't the person. We are made of so much more than two arms, two legs, a head and a brain. Our life goes beyond a heartbeat, a brain wave. The essence of each person, the soul or spirit or life force, is the real person. And that doesn't just stop. It doesn't disappear when the body gives out. That soul, that spirit, is true energy...and we know that although energy changes form, it continues on. And I have no reason to believe that the energy, the life force of an animal, doesn't go on in the same way. In fact, there are several places in scripture alluding to animals that lend support to my own beliefs.

What is really important to me, however, comes from my own experience which I shared in Part I of this book. I knew, not just felt or thought, but I *KNEW* deep, deep inside me, the moment Princess' heart stopped beating that there was no death. I remember then, as now, thinking, *"If this is dying, then I don't know what there is to be afraid of."* Holding her in my arms she quietly and softly laid her head and neck along my arm and transcended this life. I only wish there was some way to express in words the "knowing" that was mine. But it goes beyond words. For Princess, death wasn't really death at all. It was going home. It was a step through the door to the other side of life. It was release from a tired, diseased body that could only cause her pain. In my mind, there is no such thing as death, rather it is a transition from one life form to another, much like a caterpillar entering a cocoon and emerging a beautiful, free butterfly. In a very real sense, I haven't lost Princess. When you know where someone is, you haven't lost them.

Through this whole process, I have had a new awareness of just how much death is a part of life. The gift of life is inseparably linked with the promise of physical death. On no other terms do we receive the gift of life as we know it in human form. Yet, death isn't the end. I have now come to fully accept death as a transition when in an instant of time, like the butterfly, new life emerges.

Even knowing and believing that life goes on, we cannot escape the pain, the sorrow and the grieving. We miss our pet and the loss tears us apart. It is then we must remember, even if our faith is a little shaky at that moment, that God is the God of all comfort. He doesn't leave us in our times of sorrow. In fact, He is personally involved. It is then we must try, even if we can only hold to this for short moments at a time, to see our beloved pet no longer ill, no longer suffering, but transformed and renewed into wholeness.

The turning point in my healing came when I asked God for His presence and His power in my life to be willing to let go of the pain and be an open channel for healing to begin. When my own strength was washed away like sand on the ocean shore, I found a greater strength in His power that never fades. Pain reduced me to a level of total dependence on God. I am not all knowing or understanding, nor do I have an infinite amount of strength...but God does. Isaiah 43:2 captures the spirit well:

When you pass through the water, I will be with you; in the rivers you shall not drown. When you walk through the fire you shall not be burned, the flames will not consume you.

If you, too, have a strong faith as I do, and if you've just lost your pet to physical death, maybe God seems distant to you right now. You may feel He is far away, uninvolved, but He is there to comfort you if you'll accept it. He wants to support you in your loss and pain. His arms are open in love, not closed. "Come unto me and I will give you rest," Jesus said. And who needs rest more than you and me, right now, when our hearts are worn out by wrenching grief and floods of tears.

Scripture tells us that weeping may endure for a night, but joy comes in the morning. With faith, the joy becomes far more than just getting through the loss. It means being happy again *BECAUSE* you have loved. To live in faith does not mean that you will go through your loss without scars. Nor does it mean that you will ever stop missing your pet, or that you will ever totally get over the hurt. It does promise strength, however, that one day you will walk again in the light of the morning and the joy of the dawn.

Princess,
You're gone from this life, but your spirit lives on,
  Now I carry you with me, my heart sings your
  song.
I'll always miss you for time can't erase
  The love in my heart, yes, your own special place.
I talk to you often, can you hear me up there?
  I know that you do through the power of prayer.
Princess, you know that I love you, you're missed
  every day
  But now you're with God and I safely can say
You're happy and healthy and whole once again.
  And I know you live on,
  There was really no end.

TO EACH OF YOU...

There are no guarantees and time does run out. Don't assume that you have infinite years ahead to do all that you want to do or say all that you have to say. Live out your love now, in the present, and don't relinquish a certainty for the uncertainty of the future. Don't take for granted endless healing time for the bruised places and sharp edges in your relationship with your pet. Don't be afraid to be touched deeply and share openly all the sorrowful times, as well as the joyful times, because your pet is an animal and not a human.

Princess and I could never have shared enough time, enough love, enough words to have eased the pain that accompanied the grieving, but we did all that we could with the time that we had...we really lived. I didn't know exactly what I would feel or how I would be able to cope after she was gone; I just knew that I would hurt deeply and feel much pain. Perhaps not knowing was a gift in itself. Knowing would have made it even harder than it has been because I wouldn't have understood that I really would have the courage to face the pain each day, one day at a time.

Each of us must get through what we must get through, and pain and healing will come in their own time. There will be the *if onlys*. There will always be things left undone because that is a part of life. Princess and I talked of building a home in the country and I was so looking forward to having it, not just for me, but for her to enjoy where she could run and play to her heart's content. But time ran out and we'll never be able to share that together. That, too, has left me with a void, an emptiness. Now I will have to do it alone or with another pet. There will be sharing with another, but it will not diminish what Princess and I had, and still have in a very special way. No one can take her place, but there is room for another, a place in my heart that will be a different space, yet still love. It is *because* of the richness and the depth of our life together that I look forward to a new beginning. I wish to share it again.

As you grieve, as you feel the pain, welcome it and the loneliness, and it will be turned to solitude. That solitude gives you the time and space necessary for listening deeply, for finding a new peace and for discovering that you can make it in spite of your pain and your aloneness. There is no transformation without suffering; the flower does not bloom without bursting its pod.

Life without your pet will be different and the pain you feel may never entirely take its leave. But then, would you really want it to? Would you want to live without the blessing of that very special relationship? Didn't you learn from it? And didn't you learn how to love...and be loved?

No one will ever know exactly how you feel. Our relationship with our loved pets is unique. In the end, death remains a deeply personal experience. There is a certain power, a certain specialness, a certain something that no one can ever take from you in finally being able to acknowledge the experience as intimately, uniquely your own.

For you, this is my hope and my prayer: That this short book will help you take at least one step towards the joy of the morning that always follows the pain and emptiness of the night.

My love for Princess and her love for me lives on...because love was, love is and love always shall be. Her song shall continue.

That, at least, is for sure.

EPILOGUE

The first year since Princess' death has come and gone, and the second is beginning. As expected, the first anniversary, which fell on Good Friday, was a special, beautiful day of remembering, but at the same time a painful one. It was beautiful as I looked back on all the memories of the life that we shared, and very painful because I miss Princess' physical presence very much.

Today I can clearly see that the suffering I have experienced was for a reason and much has changed within me because of that suffering. It has been deeply meaningful and as I reflect on it I have come to understand that there truly can be no growth without sacrifice and suffering; that these are two of the transformational processes in life. In fact suffering, if we open ourselves to it, can open the doors to refinement. Sometimes our hearts must be broken open to find the hidden treasures inside.

The growth and deepening of love and the

spiritual realization that has been a part of my loving have helped me to understand two funda- mental experiences that are extremely significant: the union with the beloved and the terrible pain of separation. If we form membranes around our hearts that cannot be penetrated by feelings that loss and pain can bring, we close ourselves off to all that life holds. *If we can't be hurt, we can neither love nor be loved.* In the words of Rumi, a spiritual giant from ages past, who found that the way of love is the way of transformation, "Wherever there is pain, there is hope for treasure."

I have come to understand deep within that each time we die we are also reborn. I have found that as I have met the suffering consciously and allowed it to be a part of my life, it has enabled me to in some sense be opened to an emptiness that has now been filled with the ecstacy of a new and transformed union resulting from the love that Princess and I shared. Accompanying the agony and yearning for what was, a new creation has appeared and with it a renewed sense of peacefulness has now settled within me. Life will never again be the same, nor quite as simple. I can't turn back. Princess has been transformed and lives on, and now it takes the eyes of faith to recognize her. Living with Princess was to live continuously in a spirit of inspiration, and in a new way that inspiration continues today. I can't really explain it, for no words could do it justice. But I feel her with me in a new way. *Love is stronger than death.*

Perhaps in the end we shall find that the mystery of human suffering is what the mystery of transfor- mation is all about...and indeed, that love is all about both.

PENUTIAN LEGEND:

When any thing strengthens a bond of friendship,
Chimmesyans say, the friends have walked in the
shadow of a rainbow.

For the Love of Princess

Surviving the Loss of Your Pet

ORDERING INFORMATION

Additional books can be ordered for
$14.95 each, plus $2.00 shipping
and handling for the first book,
and $1.25 for each additional copy
sent to the same address.

Send check or money order to:

**Soaring Horizons® Productions
P. O. Box 25406
Portland, Oregon 97298**

www.soaringhorizons.com
www.matschek.com

About the Author.....

Cheryl Kilbourn Matschek resides in Portland, Oregon with her husband J. Norman Matschek, D.M.D. and their canine companion Daisy (a silver miniature schnauzer). Cheryl and her husband are active in the community and in their church.

Cheryl is the founder and owner of The Cheryl Matschek Company, Soaring Horizons® Productions and Princess Publishing. She is an internationally known speaker, trainer and consultant in the areas of leadership, team development, and natural health, and conducts/facilitates company retreats throughout the country.

Cheryl holds a Bachelor's degree in Psychology, Master's degree in Behavioral Science, Master's degree in Herbology and is a Certified Iridologist. She is a member of the National Speakers Association, and holds membership in a variety of other local and national organizations.

If you would like to schedule Cheryl to speak at your company or association meeting, retreat or convention, she can be contacted at The Cheryl Matschek Company, Portland, Oregon, (503) 297-1565 or FAX (503) 292-2752. Visit her websites at www.matschek.com or www.soaringhorizons.com